D1400068

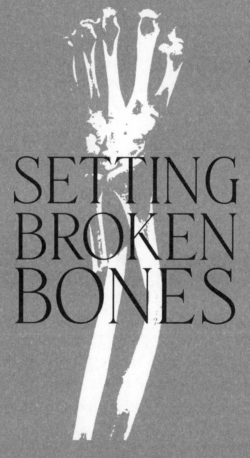

SETTING
BROKEN
BONES

SETTING BROKEN BONES

PENNY MAXWELL

CHARISMA
HOUSE

Most Charisma Media products are available at special quantity discounts for bulk purchase for sales promotions, premiums, fund-raising, and educational needs. For details, call us at (407) 333-0600 or visit our website at www. charismamedia.com.

SETTING BROKEN BONES by Penny Maxwell
Published by Charisma House, an imprint of
Charisma Media
600 Rinehart Road, Lake Mary, Florida 32746

This book or parts thereof may not be reproduced in any form, stored in a retrieval system, or transmitted in any form by any means—electronic, mechanical, photocopy, recording, or otherwise—without prior written permission of the publisher, except as provided by United States of America copyright law.

Unless otherwise noted, all Scripture quotations are taken from the Holy Bible, New International Version®, NIV®. Copyright © 1973, 1978, 1984, 2011 by Biblica, Inc.® Used by permission of Zondervan. All rights reserved worldwide. www.zondervan.com. The "NIV" and "New International Version" are trademarks registered in the United States Patent and Trademark Office by Biblica, Inc.®

Scripture quotations marked CJB are from the Complete Jewish Bible, copyright © 1998 by David H. Stern. All rights reserved.

Scripture quotations marked ESV are from the Holy Bible, English Standard Version. Copyright © 2001 by Crossway Bibles, a division of Good News Publishers. Used by permission.

Scripture quotations marked NKJV are taken from the New King James Version®. Copyright © 1982 by Thomas Nelson. Used by permission. All rights reserved.

Copyright © 2021 by Penny Maxwell
All rights reserved

Visit the author's website at FreedomHouse.cc.

Cataloging-in-Publication Data is on file with the Library of Congress.
International Standard Book Number: 978-1-63641-113-2
E-book ISBN: 978-1-63641-114-9

The author and publisher have made every effort to provide accurate accounts of events, but they acknowledge that others may have different recollections of these events. Every effort also has been made to provide accurate internet addresses at the time of publication, but neither the publisher nor the author assumes any responsibility for errors or for changes that occur after publication. Further, the publisher does not have any control over and does not assume any responsibility for author or third-party websites or their content.

21 22 23 24 25 — 987654321
Printed in the United States of America

CONTENTS

Introduction ix

Chapter 1
The Accident 1

Chapter 2
Growing Up Broken 11

Chapter 3
Leaving Hurts—and Home 31

Chapter 4
Marrying Broken 45

Chapter 5
Pandora's Box 69

Chapter 6
Barriers to Healing 83

Chapter 7
Setting Ministry Bones 99

Chapter 8
Life Hacks 119

Chapter 9
Keep on Blessing 143

Chapter 10
   The Power in Your Freedom 159

Conclusion.............................171

Epilogue................................175

Notes...................................177

INTRODUCTION

A FRIEND OF MINE once broke her nose skiing, and the nose healed improperly. It looked out of joint and crooked, and it caused her to have breathing issues at night—but she wouldn't get it fixed. Why? The doctor told her, "To fix what happened, we will have to rebreak your nose and set the bone straight." She replied, "No thanks." She didn't want to go through the pain involved in correcting the improper healing. So she dealt with the problems her crooked nose caused her.

Chances are you've had a broken bone before. Maybe you stubbed a toe or jammed a finger, and it turned out to be a fracture or a break. Maybe it was a bigger bone, like an arm, a leg, or a skull. These can heal improperly if you don't have them set right. Over time, if set wrong, that finger is less useful and looks bent, that toe won't fit into your shoe, that arm won't work like it used to—or that nose on your face looks plain weird and causes you to have breathing problems.

Emotional breaks are more abundant in life than broken bones—and so is the tendency to want to ignore them and hope they heal on their own. Sometimes they do, but often it's obvious there has been a break. Still, we make excuses:

"I'll get it looked at later."

"I'll wait until it causes me problems."

"I didn't need it to work perfectly anyway."

"I'll manage. I have up to now."

But by living with it, we lose functionality. We suffer emotionally. Things don't fit and don't work, and we wonder why. Or maybe we know why, and we still ignore it.

Inside we are crooked, and this shows up in our relationships, in our thought lives, in the words that come out of our mouths. We all would like to pretend that nobody can see our brokenness or that we manage it well. We cram the crooked finger into a glove or the crooked toe into a shoe and hide our nonfunctionality and our pain. But in many cases we can't sleep at night. We are spiritually unable to breathe.

Sometimes the pain is sharp, the memory fresh, the feeling persistent. Or maybe the hurts are so familiar—and so abundant—that you're not exactly sure what is causing them anymore. But under the surface these wrongly set fractures remain. And they are hindering your progress. It's hard to do life with bones that healed crookedly. So many people try to press through, to get along, to smile, to fake it till they make it to a place of healing. That approach, I can promise you, is pretty useless. Picture going to the emergency room with a broken arm and not letting the doctors or nurses touch it. It wouldn't matter where you were if you denied their help. So many Christians live that way—they show up to church, serve regularly, and praise wholeheartedly. But when God reaches out to touch their broken spots, they pull back. They don't want to feel the brokenness again. They'd rather hope it goes away on its own.

It won't.

Only God can heal and reset our broken places, and by hard experience I have learned how to cooperate with Him in the process. I have lived in that place of sharp, continuing pain that clouded my emotions and stole my ability to trust anyone. So much happened to me that most of my emotional bones were broken by the time I left home as a teenager. Thankfully I received God's mercy toward the broken. My journey has shown me firsthand how God resets our broken bones so they heal up. That way we can move on in wholeness, peace, and personal fulfillment. I want to share how you can do this too.

How bad does your situation have to be before you agree to be healed? How long will you limp through life before deciding it's worth the discomfort and outright pain to heal the way Jesus intended you to heal?

Now is your time. You can heal right. I know because I did.

One thing before we get started: please stick with your healing all the way through. Don't bail out just because it feels rough sometimes. God has a destination for you, a better place to be. In fact that place is the start of a new experience of life with Him and with people around you. I know you can make it, because I did. Decide now to travel all the way to the end, where you will find a brand-new beginning.

Let's reset those broken bones.

—Penny Maxwell
Charlotte, North Carolina
August 2021

CHAPTER 1

THE ACCIDENT

Y OU DON'T GET many calls like the one I got right after a meeting with our church staff in the living room of our home. At the start of every year, we cast vision, dream together, and imagine what God has next for our church. It's an invigorating, focusing time that helps launch us into the new year. I was enjoying the afterglow of that while tidying up when a call instantly dispelled all good feelings.

"Colby's been in an accident," the caller said, referring to my and my husband, Troy's son and oldest child. "It was bad—real bad."

It's amazing how fast your body and mind can go numb. The warmth of our just-ended staff leadership meeting vanished; in its place was an icy river of doubts and questions: "What kind of an accident?

How bad was it? Was Colby injured? Was anyone else injured? Where is my son now?"

The tingling that initially coursed through my body gave way to frozen fear. I must have said something, but I can't remember what. I hung up and called Troy, who said he would meet me at the location of the accident as soon as he could. Without even grabbing my usual things, I went out to my car, started it, and began driving.

"Lord, please let Colby be safe," I prayed as I backed out of our driveway and sped toward the scene. I was in that zone you find yourself in when the very worst possibilities may become actual. Seconds felt like hours as I guided the car through familiar roads near our home in Charlotte. The cold, sunny day had a hardness to it—an unyielding reality that I couldn't hide from.

Something had happened to Colby; I was about to face it.

The irony of the timing was not lost on me. Staff members and I had just spent a couple of hours writing ideas on a big sheet of paper on an easel in our house. One of the things I was doing around the time the call came was transferring those notes to an electronic document. It was like someone had taken the list of our hopes and dreams and torn it in two.

Now I heard sirens. Lots of sirens. I wasn't even halfway there.

"Oh, God," I prayed, "this sounds really big."

A wall of traffic soon stood before me. A snaky line of brake lights backed up onto the main roads. Nobody was going anywhere. In my mind questions collided: "How am I going to get to him with all this traffic? What will I see when I get there?"

I had no qualms about going off road in my urban-mama SUV, knowing that if I got pulled over, I would at least gain a police escort. Onto the shoulder I steered the car, bumping past hundreds of waiting vehicles. Then the shoulder ran out.

Even though I was dressed in business clothes and high heels—it hadn't occurred to me to waste time grabbing a coat or changing my shoes before I went out the door—I couldn't just sit in my car and wait. I didn't hesitate one second but parked on a convenient side road, jumped out, yanked my high heels off, and started half jogging in my bare feet on the asphalt. An open lane stood before me, where oncoming traffic would have been. To my right was the endless line of people having a normal day as they headed home. I was the one in crisis now, tracing the path that would take me to see whether my son was still alive. It was the longest mile of my life.

Walking barefoot for what seemed like a separate lifetime brought me within sight of the grim destination. Cars had flipped upside down; some clearly would never be salvaged except for parts. Ambulances and fire trucks sat zigzag, harsh lights strobing the scene. I recognized that one of the upside-down cars belonged to Colby. Around it a veil of broken glass shimmered from the ground.

"God, I beg You for mercy," my heart cried. I strained my eyes to find our son, hoping he was alive.

⌒

The loss of my oldest child would certainly be the most difficult thing I would have had to overcome in my forty-(mumble) years. Like any parent I could not imagine worse news. But something told me I had the strength for whatever I encountered. I had traveled long roads of healing before. Sexually, physically, and emotionally abused as a child, I had navigated a way to a healthy life, marriage, and ministry without much baggage. That had taken a lot of work—really unpleasant but necessary work—yet I could say by God's grace I had overcome. He really is greater than anything that happens to us. I saw many people fall by the wayside and never make it through tough things. But God had proved Himself faithful over and over again—every time. He would do it again, no matter what the circumstance held.

Meanwhile Troy was on his way with an off-duty policeman in our city who had recognized our car at the center of an accident on a notoriously curvy road about eight miles from our house. As I stepped nearer, I could see stretchers on the ground. My eyes darted to each one. Colby's form wasn't on any of them.

Instead of being thankful, my mind spun through the worst possibilities.

"Is he on the ground somewhere with a cloth over him? Or is he still in his car after all this time?" I didn't have to wonder long. As I picked my way through the scene, suddenly I spotted him. He was standing on the embankment. My mother's heart seemed to burst as I rushed over to him.

"Are you OK?" I asked, grabbing hold of him carefully. I could see he had bruises by the way he was holding himself.

"Yeah, I'm fine," he said in typical seventeen-year-old-male fashion. "I crawled out through the broken windshield. Those airbags hurt."

He winced in pain from a bruise beneath his shirt somewhere. I was so overwhelmed to see him standing before me alive that I couldn't cry or react. My mind had begun to recalibrate around worse possibilities. Hope returned like the tide, slowly but inevitably.

A police officer came up to talk with me. He had been interviewing people.

"Ma'am," he said, "this right here is called Dead Man's Curve. We don't have accidents here where the coroner doesn't come. This is a first for us. It's a miracle that everybody is walking away from this with their lives."

As with everything at that moment, I took in his words mostly without expression of outward emotion.

Then he and Colby stepped aside for an interview about what had happened. I stood on that knoll alone, watching the evolving scene. Crews were cleaning up glass. Some victims had been loaded into ambulances. The worst was over.

That's when the Lord spoke to me specifically and clearly.

"Do you trust Me?" He said.

Gratitude practically poured from my soul in response.

"Lord, You know I trust You. You just saved my son's life. This could have been so different," I said inwardly.

"That's not what I'm asking you," He replied. "Do you trust Me?"

Now He was meddling, and I protested a bit, "Lord, he shouldn't have walked away from this. Of course I trust You."

But He wasn't done.

"If it hadn't worked out the way it did, and you weren't taking your son home with you, would you still trust Me?" He pressed in His gentle but unyielding way.

Now I grew perturbed.

"Why in the world are we having this conversation now?" I fumed at the Lord. I've never been afraid to express my true emotions to Him. There I stood, watching the cleanup process of an accident that could have—should have, according to the officer—taken my son's life. "Can't You see I'm a little traumatized?" I continued. "I almost lost my son."

Whenever I push, He always pushes back harder.

"Because I need to hear your answer before you come off this hill, or every single day when one of your children leaves the house, you will look out the window and wonder if they are coming back," He said to my heart. "If you don't trust Me and crucify your fear at this moment, that fear will be present all the time. You will replay this over and over."

I was still miffed that He was dealing with me so firmly in such a sensitive moment. Yet I knew His timing, like His love, was perfect. So I listened.

"I am a good God not because Colby is walking away from this," He continued. "I am a good God because I am faithful. Faithful doesn't always look like getting the answer you like. I was in the midst of this. I was in the car, and I am in every situation, even when it's painful and difficult."

This was all true, but I wasn't going to answer quickly or untruthfully. I needed to sit with this one for a moment. I still had two younger kids who didn't have their driver's licenses yet—they were both home when I dashed out the door. Like any mom, the two main things I worried about—pardon me, *prayed* about—were that I would never do anything to mess up my kids and that they would suffer no harm in instances like this. The first one I had some control over; the second one I didn't. Would I affirm that I trusted a good God whatever future outcomes might be? Or would my trust be situational and outcome based?

I wanted to say yes to the first question, but I didn't want to verbalize it. It felt like sitting in an emergency row on an airplane when the steward asks, "Are you willing to assist in an emergency?" Just nodding your head doesn't count. They tell you, "I need a verbal *yes*." I was nodding my head to God, but I felt as if He was saying, "That's not enough. I need a verbal *yes*."

So I said it.

"Yes, God. I trust You. I will give You full rein in my heart. I give You everything. I promise that even if I weren't walking away with my son alive, my faith is in You alone."

This was nonnegotiable. I was giving Him full access to my heart, risking great pain. But I had made my choice.

The officer was done interviewing Colby. Troy had just arrived. There wasn't anything left to do but go home, but before we did, I took a photo of the accident scene to remember God's faithfulness.

⌒

So much had transpired in my heart and mind since I last set foot in my own living room. The easel was still there from the meeting, but as I looked closer, I saw that my two young girls had removed the top page, with all the vision statements and ideas, and had filled the next page with statements of God's truth over Colby's accident. Atop the page the girls wrote, "Fear vs. God. We're going to give you a visual representation."

The word *fear* they wrote very small, along with the word *microscopic*. By the word God they wrote *infinitive*. (They meant *infinite*.) Further they expounded, "God is much bigger. God is infinitive. Fear is a thought. Fear is from the devil and you shouldn't listen to the devil anyways. Fear isn't real. It's real unless you tell yourself otherwise which is something you should do. Don't be fearful of things you know can't happen to you."

In a new color of marker they wrote, "Fear is dumb. Sorry/not sorry, devil."

That was the perfect summary of what God had told me on the mound by the accident site. Fear is dumb. Fear is useless. Fear needs to be broken.

We had our son back without so much as a broken bone, but I had crossed a bridge of commitment with God that would prove again how He was faithful—even when life brought disasters.

CHAPTER 2

GROWING UP BROKEN

YOU WOULDN'T HAVE liked my childhood any more than I did.

I'll sum it up this way: At first my family was poor and quite miserable. Then great pain hit me like a freight train. Then we became quite rich and were still miserable. Then I left home.

Like a lot of people, I had to forgive nearly every important adult in my life for doing some really hurtful stuff. Half healed, I launched into independence as soon as I could, scurrying away from the harm and the pain that had marred my childhood home. Out there alone I was perfectly poised for a whole bunch of bone resetting I didn't know I needed because so much had been shattered.

I was about to find out exactly what was wrong with me.

DINNER WITH DARRYL

One evening Troy and I were at dinner with a family friend, Darryl Strawberry. Darryl lived through a kind of public humiliation—much of it self-induced—during his Major League Baseball career. Hookers and drugs, all kinds of addiction, nasty headlines, shame, suspensions, restorations, and new failures plagued his young adult years. But Darryl walked out of that gnarly experience a healed man. How did he do that? I asked him that night, "Why did you and I successfully walk through all the traumas of our past, but so many people don't?"

His response was instant: "It's because they're not willing to go through the pain."

I knew it was true, though it has taken me years to understand the depth of this statement. My own observation as a copastor of a church and in decades of ministry has shown me repeatedly that some people just aren't willing to heal from bad things that happen to them. They go through life angry, with broken bones that hurt anytime someone jostles them or gets in their way. These walking wounded live the lie that somehow Jesus' sacrifice doesn't offer full restoration for them. But Jesus' power to heal us is the only guarantee that we will heal. And we will. When He's in charge, He never fails.

But we have to let Him take the lead.

A Blue Pinto and a Church Bus

My unmarried mother got pregnant with me in 1971 three months after giving birth to my half brother, who was the son of another man. Facing a whole heap of potentially public shame, Mom could have given in to the pressure from my biological father to have me aborted. Instead, she was able to persuade him to marry her, support my birth, adopt my half brother, and pretend that both of us were his own. I can only assume he did this so that my mother's indiscretions would remain unknown. Their marriage ended rather quickly, and my slightly older brother and I grew up with Mom, thinking we had the same father. Over the next few decades, my two biological parents would end up with eight marriages between them. In my opinion, they were heartache factories and unhappy people.

My first memories are of Mom, my brother, and me living in a small run-down first-floor apartment, where I remember seeing her boyfriends come and go through our door. Our car was a baby-blue Ford Pinto that barely kept running. I remember her eating potato chips, or something like it, for dinner, and it always seemed that if something good happened to us, it was because my grandparents were behind it. They gave Mom money and bought clothes and things for us.

Mom worked, so my brother and I took the bus to

an after-school day care program. Later she switched us to an after-school babysitter, and the bus dropped us off at the babysitter's house. On so many pleasant afternoons I sat in another room of this house while the mother worked with her girls on their homework. I thought how wonderful it would be to have a mom who did homework with me—or was even home when school let out. Every evening, this house became filled with amazing aromas of dinners this mother made for her family. I was absolutely transported by the smells and even more by the fact that these people got to sit down and eat a meal together as a family. The twice-baked potatoes she made one evening stuck in my young mind as the gold standard of family togetherness and love. I included a recipe for them in my cookbook later in life.

One time we went with the babysitter to a dentist's office—my first visit to such a place. The babysitter was surprised we had never had our teeth looked at, and this accentuated the growing feeling that my family was less than, different, and even possibly poor.

One Sunday morning a church bus rumbled up to our apartment complex, and Mom let me get on that bus by myself to attend a little Baptist church. She didn't come, and neither did my brother, but from that point on I didn't miss that bus. Church was the happiest place I knew. In kids' church I said my memory verse and got candy. Everybody was nice to me and to everyone else. From that time on—perhaps even before then—I never had to be convinced that God was real and that I loved Him. I was only four years old, and while there were pieces of my life that I didn't understand, what I felt on that bus and what I heard at the neighborhood church made heart sense to me.

For the most part, by contrast, our home felt joyless. I did not feel safe or protected in my bedroom but isolated. I can recall sitting on my bed, examining the marks on my legs after one of our family explosions. Sometimes the marks on my legs showed the outline of a belt strap and holes. It didn't bother me because I thought this was the same for every girl. I didn't know to be ashamed of it, and I'm not sure I would have hidden it anyway. I remember one time when a family member noticed the marks and mentioned them to my mom, but it didn't change much. Neither my bedroom nor anywhere else in the apartment ever felt safe.

Because of my developing need to feel protected and loved, my heart went out to anyone in need and especially to those who were bullied at school. I stepped in and looked out for people when others picked on them, and anytime I saw a neighbor in need, I rushed to help however I could. This brought me joy.

So did Jerry's Kids. Every year, the popular money-raising telethon starring Jerry Lewis consumed my attention. I was taken by the fact that people would rally around very needy children. I absolutely loved it, and I would grab my Maxwell House coffee can (with no idea how prophetic that brand name actually was) and go door-to-door collecting money. I believed deeply in the cause.

One Saturday morning a lady opened her door and listened as I asked if she would like to support Jerry's Kids. I held the Maxwell House can up.

"Why would a young girl like you spend a Saturday doing this?" she asked me (but not meanly).

"I couldn't think of anything better to do," I said honestly and then pressed my pitch. "If you're not comfortable giving cash, you can write a check to the organization."

She paused and then said, "I'll be right back." She came back with a check for ten dollars, which I stuffed into the can with the pile of change already clanking around in there.

Each year, I anticipated taking the money I had collected to the drop site, where you got to dump all your money into big fish tanks, and they showed this on live TV. It was thrilling to me.

MYRTLE BEACH

Relationships didn't seem to be Mom's strong point. One experience summed this up vividly in those early years. I don't remember where my brother was, but Mom and some guy she was dating took me with them on a trip to a condo in Myrtle Beach. It was what people now call a breakup trip, but that was way beyond my understanding at the time. All I remember is that they began fighting, and things got out of control, emotionally and physically. I was clearly in the way, and because they wanted time alone to have a conversation—or a fight—the man's parents arrived to take me out for a little while. These were perfect strangers to me, though not unpleasant-seeming people. Still, I didn't want to go. His father did a couple of coin tricks—taking a coin out of my ear, for example—to build a bridge, but I was four years old and not ready to go anywhere with people I'd never seen before.

"Listen, she doesn't know us. It's not right to force her," I remember the mother saying as I cried and cried. When they left and it was just the three of us again, I remember Mom putting me in a closet.

"You can't come out," she said. "I'm having a grown-up conversation."

Of course I came out and saw her crying too. Then she put me on the balcony. It was dark, and the wind was blowing. I heard her lock the sliding glass door and saw her close the curtain. Thank goodness I don't remember how long I was out there while in that sad room their relationship dissolved.

DAD

My biological dad's charm and charisma could command an entire room, but he had no moral compass whatsoever, as far as I could detect. He drank heavily, drove a sporty GTO car, and was able to function well enough to work even after downing most of a bottle of Jack Daniel's whiskey.

In his closet at his apartment he hung his T-shirts neatly and in order. He wore only T-shirts and jeans, and at times, I flipped through the shirts and tried to read the words and understand the meanings. In time it dawned on me that every single one of them was vulgar and some were graphic. Many bore curse words. As a rather innocent little girl I was dumbfounded that my father wore such off-color shirts. Yet this was his daily garb.

I usually visited him once a year, at Christmas, and one year he was talking about the fact that my brother was dealing with acne. As usual Dad was drunk.

"I'm really concerned that in a year I'll struggle with acne too because my brother is," I said.

Dad smiled knowingly and said, "Sweetheart, you don't ever need to worry about that. You won't have to deal with acne."

"You don't know that," I responded.

"Kid, you come from good stock. Don't worry about it," he said.

"What are you talking about?" I asked.

"PJ," he said to me, using my nickname, which was short for Penny Jean, "your brother is adopted. I adopted him to save face for your mother."

"He's just drunk," I thought, and ignored it.

Two weeks later my brother and I got into an

argument over something in the backyard. It escalated into a full-on shouting match until I yelled, "Oh yeah? Well, you're adopted!"

Out of nowhere the back door flew open, and Mom bolted out. From her outburst I knew she was extremely angry with me. All I could think was, "I've said way worse things than that. Why am I getting beat up over this?"

Of course I had always noticed that my brother and I are the opposite in every way. We don't look alike, act alike, or have the same interests, but Mom always accused me of making up lies about those supposed differences. As she flew into a rage, she seemed intent on making sure I would never mention it again.

A few years earlier, when I was ten, I was walking to some friends' houses and stopped by a girl's house along the way. We stood there talking at the front door, and she asked where I was going.

"Over to Richard and David's," I said simply. "We're going to shoot basketballs."

That was it, but later this girl divulged something to me.

"You know, your mom and my mom went to high school together," she said. "When you were going to Richard and David's house, my mom said, 'She's growing up just like her mama then.'"

I couldn't grasp what that meant, but it seemed to explain the men who came and went from our house, Mom's need for approval, and even the way she dressed at times. Pieces of my family history were coming into view.

At a young age I also began a complex relationship with food. When nothing else brought comfort, food did. That's not uncommon in the South, where comfort food originated. For me it provided an escape from harsh realities. I didn't know that when food is not in its proper place in your life, it can cause problems. Food also became a contest of wills between my mother and me. The house rule was that you ate whatever was put in front of you, and you didn't get up from the table until your plate was clean. The problem was there were a lot of foods I didn't like. Looking back, I realize that Mom didn't seem to know how to prepare food, or she just didn't take the time. More than one awful night, I sat there with the eleven o'clock news on the TV and a plate of slimy asparagus straight from the can in front of me.

How to have a good relationship with food—that would be a great subject for a book all its own.

My Grandfather, the Abuser

By this time, my grandfather had been sexually abusing me for years. Of course I didn't understand what was going on. I just knew I couldn't trust him, and I did all I could to avoid being near him.

School was a safe place. I wasn't an over-the-top-excellent student, but I loved being with people, talking with people, and helping people. If my teacher needed assistance, I was the first to jump in. School felt like level ground. Nothing harmful could reach me there.

But if I wasn't feeling well, my mother would call my grandfather to pick me up, and I knew what that meant. So I went to school even if I felt sick and tried to hold it together. This didn't always work. One day in third grade my teacher noticed I wasn't feeling well, though I insisted, "I feel fine." There was no way I was going home if I could help it, because I knew what would happen to me there. My teacher had me sit in the hallway, and there I threw up all over the place. So she sent me to the nurse's office.

Crying, I kept saying, "I feel good. It was an accident. I didn't mean it."

But it didn't help. The next thing I knew, my grandfather was in the nurse's office to pick me up. You can guess what happened after that.

Since those days at the Baptist church, I had truly loved God, and while I didn't understand why I had to go through things I did, I never blamed God for them. I knew that individual people had power to make choices, even wrong ones. I certainly asked, "Why?" a lot and wondered why people didn't protect me. But I didn't point the finger at God.

A little wooden cross with a rawhide strap hung on my bedpost. Every night, I put it over my neck as I went to bed and prayed, "God, I know You're there. I don't know why all this is happening." That cross necklace and that routine gave me comfort. I knew that as bad as everything was, it wasn't God's fault. While I slept, the cross lay against my neck like a promise of a better future.

MOVING ON UP

When I was in grade school, Mom met and married a man—her third time walking down the aisle—and this marriage lasted. It also occasioned a big change in our standard of living because this man had money.

We moved from our shabby apartment to a beautiful brick home in the nice area of Richmond known as Bon Air. Overnight our original trio—Mom, my brother, and I—went from poor to wealthy. Our new stepfather was an entrepreneurial businessman who seemed concerned only about his work and starting a new business. There wasn't a lot of connection or warmth there. Home from work, he sat in an easy chair, put his feet up, and read the paper. We soon learned to leave him alone because our presence as kids seemed to irritate him. He wasn't mean or abusive, but he certainly wasn't the fatherly, climb-up-in-his-lap-and-cuddle type.

A number of times, I had trouble with math homework and asked for his help because he was brilliant with numbers. In each instance, he became really annoyed and didn't want to deal with it. I figured that was how all adults felt, that kids were an interruption. That coldness aside, my stepfather was a good provider, and he wasn't physically abusive. He didn't scream and yell. I concluded that the fact that he provided for us and wasn't beating me up made him a good person.

But money can't solve heart issues. In fact it seems to magnify them. It didn't appear to me that it made Mom any happier; rather, her unhappiness extended to money, which seemed to enlarge it. One major point of contention between her and my stepfather was that he wanted her to keep working while he was starting a new business. She did this very grudgingly and came home from her job as a secretary every day complaining about how horrible her boss was and recounting the negative characteristics of everyone she worked with. By contrast she was a hero in all her stories, playing the role of an amazing saint in an office full of terrible people.

I think she resented her new husband's devotion to his work and felt less cared for as a result of it. "His job is the other woman," she would say, and since this anger had to go somewhere, it usually fell on me.

I'm not trying to paint an unnecessarily ugly picture. Many people I have talked to experienced worse than I did—cracked ribs, busted jaws, hospitalizations, and cover-ups. Some wonder why such people don't simply walk out of those situations and never go back. I know why—it's because you think it's normal. My whole family was dysfunctional, and I assumed that was how everything was. As a kid you tend to define the world by what you experience and by what your parents tell you. My mom was such a master manipulator that anything she did to me was always going to end up being my fault. I can remember her saying things such as, "It's your fault. If you weren't such a bad kid, I wouldn't have to do this."

I thought, "Wow, I am a bad kid. I talked back."

This was my normal, and in my young mind it happened because of me.

The more our family had in terms of possessions, the more Mom seemed manic to control it all. Every inch of the house had to be spotless, and much of this responsibility fell to me. Mom would come behind me to monitor how clean things were, and if I didn't leave things perfect, I paid for it. If I laid my toothbrush down by the sink for two seconds to rinse my mouth, she yelled at me. If dishes were not put in the dishwasher properly, if the spoon and knife were not turned the proper way in the dishwasher basket, or if I left any item in an unapproved location in the house—all of this was cause for instant rage.

One time Mom put her hand behind the headboard of my bed, swiped, and said, "There's dust there." Mind you, this part of the bed was up against the wall, was not visible, and was never touched. But it had to be kept clean, just like everything else.

One morning as I got ready to head to school, I left the sheet hanging below the comforter and didn't catch it. This was a major transgression because I was taught to make beds look perfect, with the zippers on the pillows facing downward, the stripes on the sheets going the right way, and so on. Mom went in behind me, as she always did, to inspect my room before I left. She was so furious to see the drooping sheet that she ripped all the blankets and sheets off the bed.

"You did that on purpose," she said. "You're taunting me."

I thought, "Why would I do that to you? I spend my life trying not to make you angry."

My brother, the only other normal person in my family, as far as I was concerned, was far more compliant at a younger age. He had a relaxed personality and didn't speak up against the wrongs in our household until years later. When we were young, he learned to play the game, and he would instruct me, "Penny, if you just let this happen, and do this, and don't do this, things will be better."

But even he didn't escape Mom's instant wrath at times. One time, he was walking up the steps with a pickle in his hand—yes, a pickle. Mom had an iron rule that food was never to leave the kitchen. Mom passed him, saw the pickle, and instantly flew into a rage.

"How dare you break my rules!" she demanded.

But she was usually far less forceful with him than she was with me, and it seemed that part of it was her insecurity and jealousy of women generally, even extending to me. But I now believe the main driver was something neither my brother nor I really understood at the time: we had different fathers, my father had cheated on my mom many times, and she had never forgiven him for it—and I looked like him.

To make it worse, my dad knew my brother was not his son, and Mom was pretending that he was. This secret seemed to hang over Mom's head like a silent threat.

As I got older, the difference in treatment became more obvious, and one time I went to her crying and said, "Why are you so mean to me? You're not mean to my brother. What is wrong with me? Why am I always the one? You like him better than me."

"That's just the devil talking to you," she replied. "He's in your head."

I was just trying to make sense of everything I was seeing. It looked to me as if Mom blamed my dad for anything that went wrong with us. In fact she made us call my biological father by his first name, Gene, while we had to call our stepfather Dad. No matter what she made us call them, it was obvious to me that she liked my brother better, and Gene liked me better. She wouldn't admit the truth about our different dads until we were nearly adults.

When I was a child, my stepfather always provided financially, but I always felt a shortage of love. As an adult I never had a hard time believing that God could come through financially when I needed it, because that was something I had experienced, but I did struggle to believe that God could love me unconditionally, because I never saw that modeled in my life. Love was conditional: if you clean this or get a good grade or behave, I approve of you and celebrate you. I figured God must be that way too.

What destabilized my heart the most—even more than the sexual abuse—was the up-and-down, inconsistent nature of Mom's moods. Waking up, I never knew if it would be a good day or a disastrous day. I might come into the kitchen and hear, "Sweetheart, I made your favorite breakfast today." I can only assume that part of this was Mom feeling the pressure to keep up appearances based on how other wealthy people behaved. She played the part, all prim and proper and telling me, "Hi, darling!"

I was like, "I sure wasn't 'darling' yesterday."

The next day I would wake up to a sharp, "You're going to sit down and eat this food and not get up until I tell you to." She knew the foods I didn't like, and it sure seemed she made them intentionally and went to war with me over them. That's when I knew what kind of day it would be.

Penance gifts appeared throughout the cycle. Some days I would come home from school and see a new outfit lying across my bed, and I knew it was an apology for what she had done the day before. I wanted to believe that Mom's heart had truly changed and that she wouldn't hurt me anymore. But the cycle continued. Outbursts and attacks, blaming me, gifts and sweetness, and then around the circle again.

A number of friends told me they were envious of my lifestyle at this stage because I seemed to have it all. I had my own phone line with my own phone number, a very nice stereo system with big speakers, and a TV in my room. I was rich in guilt gifts from Mom. My friends didn't know—and I didn't tell them—that I would have given up any or all of it— the big house, TV, stereo, and phone line—to have a healthy family to grow up in. This was emphasized in my mind when Mom used the gifts to control me: "If you don't obey me, I'm taking your phone or your TV." The lesson I took from that—and it was actually a good one—was never to let my heart attach to material things.

I can say honestly that having wealth during that time in my life taught me two good things: First, my Father in heaven will always care for me. Provision is not a problem for Him. Second, money and things are just not that important. Relationships are. They are the true treasure. At the time, I had little of that treasure.

Protecting the Abuser

The truth about my grandfather began coming out just before I entered my teens, and I told my mother what my grandfather had been doing to me for years. But rather than shelter me and hold him to account,

Mom seemed to be embarrassed, and my grand-mother wouldn't believe me. I even remember them blaming me for causing shame and division in the family. But I couldn't overlook things just to keep peace.

The eruption of this information into our lives changed the way holidays looked. Our relatives wouldn't get together anymore, and I was made to feel at fault. Even then I knew that their response wasn't right, but it was hurtful and confusing that nobody was feeling the weight of what my grandfather had done. My stepfather played the ostrich with his head in the sand. My grandmother played cover-up for the family dysfunction, accusing me of lying about what I had suffered at the hands of her husband. Only when other victims came forward did she have to face the truth.

There was a public trial, and I had to take the wit-ness stand and literally point at my grandfather to identify him as my abuser. He was found guilty and sentenced to jail time, but the climate was different than it is today, and my mom intervened to bail him out. I think she felt bad for him because he was curled up in a fetal position in his brief time in a cell. She made every excuse in the book for him. I can only assume this was in an effort to restore his reputation, which was key to keeping her own. In response to her bailing him out, the judge said to my grandfather, "Sir, if you ever come back to my courtroom for this or any other infraction, I will add this penalty on to it. I find you pitiful." So my abuser was convicted but served no time.

It may sound hard to believe, but the sexual abuse was not what harmed me most from my childhood. The hardest thing was having Jekyll and Hyde for a mother. The unpredictability caused crippling anxiety. With my grandfather I knew exactly what was going to happen. There were no surprises. But with my mother I never knew if she was going to lash out at me or praise me.

My grandfather's abuse of me had ended, and something just as big was about to happen: Mom was about to get saved.

CHAPTER 3

LEAVING HURTS—AND HOME

A T SOME POINT Mom developed a medical condition, and it was serious. After moving to Bon Air, we had begun attending church, and the leaders there told Mom it was God's will for her to have this condition. If she died, she died. Somehow whatever happened to people was God's will and could not be avoided, according to their view.

Mom got tired of hearing that and began searching for a place that actually believed God could heal. She found a new kind of church for us—a large Spirit-filled church. Gone were the hymns and the organ. This place had a rock-style band, overhead projectors, and loud, upbeat music. People really seemed to believe and live what they sang and preached. Mom took us there week after week, though our stepfather wasn't enthusiastic about attending.

I plugged into the youth group, though in my snobby view the kids there weren't very cool. But I was hearing about a powerful God, and the teaching started to sink in.

By this time, I had seen enough of the world to form the opinion that Mom was nuts. As great as it was that she no longer drank, smoked, and cussed the way I remembered her doing when I was younger, she developed a set of sanctified vices including perfectionism and pride that now ruled the household. Overnight, Mom seemed to become a version of the model Christian woman. I always felt she made strong judgments about how unholy and unrighteous other people were and how no one could hear God the way she could. Of course I wanted my mom to hear from God; I just wanted her to realize that other people did too. And the outbursts and attacks she directed toward me never went away but now took on a holy veneer.

The restrictions she placed on us became religious rather than just random. For example, I was not allowed to attend my high school baccalaureate because it was held in a Baptist church and in her view they were not as holy as she was. My Jewish friend wasn't allowed to park his car in our driveway or come into our house. If I wanted to hang out with him, I had to walk down the street, and he would pick me up.

This new set of rules, combined with my own desire

to be independent from all of it, drove me to do as much as I could outside our house. I often quipped that we didn't have a home; we had a mausoleum.

STAYING AWAY

In my preteen years I had started babysitting so I could have my own money because I didn't like the way Mom used possessions to manipulate me. She frequently threatened to throw me out of the house if I disobeyed, and once she actually did throw all my stuff on the driveway. I was fourteen.

When I turned fifteen, I got a worker's permit so I could spend more time away from home and earn my freedom. My job was at a high-fashion boutique. It was everything I loved: fashion, clothing, and the art of it all. Richmond was home to a world-renowned art school, and there was something of a fashion culture in town. At the store they let me dress the mannequins and coordinate their outfits. This thrilled me in every way. I also loved visiting other stores in the ritzy part of town to feel the fabrics and appreciate the different designs. I worked from 6:00 p.m. to 9:30 p.m. several times a week while in high school.

Often I went to work at the fashion boutique after softball practice. Playing fast-pitch softball had become a highlight of my school year. Before that I had really enjoyed doing gymnastics, but when Mom held it over my head and threatened to take it away, I gave it up. I was always detaching from things she used to control me. Softball gave me a reason to be out of the house. Practices were held at school, and I figured that because it was a team sport, Mom wouldn't make the whole team suffer, simply for the sake of appearances. I was right.

I wasn't a natural athlete or naturally competitive, but I grew to appreciate the strategy of the game. There were different pitches for different batters. You could steal bases and bunt. I played third base and left field. Still, at first my teammates teased me a bit because I didn't fit the softball profile. The coach admitted later that when I first tried out, "I didn't think you would be able to do this. I took one look at you, sized you up, and said, 'She won't want to get her nails or her hair dirty.'"

I helped prove her wrong one game when she gave me the signal to steal second. As I slid into the base, the catcher's throw hit me in the shoulder and my knee got tweaked. In one moment I had earned a busted knee and a big bruise on my shoulder, which was very obvious at prom the next week. In a way these injuries were a badge of honor for me.

Softball occupied my afternoons, and then I would shower, put on nice clothes, and head straight to work. The other ladies in the boutique didn't want the evening shift, but it was perfect for me. Then I went home, did homework, and went to school early the next morning. My routine of near-total absence was working very well for me.

I still visited my real dad irregularly, and he was the same as he'd always been—a charming, drinking, would-be Casanova. By this time, he was married to his fifth wife. In my senior year of high school, while I was at his house, he asked me if I knew a girl named so-and-so. I said I didn't.

"She's in your homeroom," he insisted.

"I don't know who she is. Why?" I asked.

"She's one of my girlfriends," he said casually.

"That's disgusting!" I said.

"Hey, she's eighteen," he replied.

That was how weird my life was, yet I knew there was a better way to do things. I knew there were healthy people out there who loved their wives and kids and husbands. I had glimpsed such families in places such as church but had not seen that lifestyle lived out up close in any sustained way. I was still searching desperately for it.

Stopping Mom's Manipulation

Meanwhile Mom was stricter than ever, and now she had a veneer of Holy Spirit empowerment. One of the more hurtful moments of those years came on the night of a big event I had been looking forward to for months. A Christian rock band was coming to our church, and I couldn't wait to go. I had been talking about it excitedly with my friends and even with Mom.

An hour before I was supposed to leave for the

concert, Mom discovered that I had put a pair of jeans into the dryer to shrink them.

"You're wasting electricity," she said. "You're not going tonight."

"Mom! I've been looking forward to this for so long," I protested.

"You don't just dry one item," she responded. "You're wasting electricity, and we will not do that in this house."

The night I had anticipated for so long was taken from me just like that. It was pure heartache.

One time, Mom came to me in the playroom above our garage and said, "I want you to know the Lord told me you're doing drugs. The Holy Spirit revealed that to me."

I'd had enough.

"Well, you're full of it, and I always knew you were, but this is all the confirmation I needed," I retorted. "I'm not doing drugs, unless you count the occasional Tylenol."

"Oh no," she insisted. "The Holy Spirit revealed it to me."

"The Holy Spirit didn't reveal jack to you," I said boldly. "You're flat-out lying."

It was an important moment for me because I was no longer going to be manipulated by "God said." It liberated me from fear of that phrase—a phrase I only rarely use today because it has such power to put a trip on people. But I did become more curious about spiritual things because I was motivated to figure God out for myself. I knew her version wasn't the best representation of His character. But what was?

Mom's transfer of controlling dysfunction made me realize that just because someone is in a position of authority doesn't mean that person is necessarily dependable. I had to learn to hear God for myself and get in a relationship with Him. I remember thinking, "I can't trust what other people say. I've got to make sure I've got a word from God." That's why Troy and I in crazy times stay the course and don't get caught up in what everybody says. For example, people actually told us not to start Freedom House Church. They said things such as, "Why would you guys do that? You have great jobs and a great family."

But as I like to say, when you have a word from God, every decision becomes an easy decision. Some people might look at what you're choosing to do and think, "That's hard," but if you have a word from God, it's not hard, and it doesn't matter what people—even spiritual people—say against it. I developed that skill by learning early on that not everybody is trustworthy, but God is, and I needed to hear from Him.

I had started teaching a Sunday school class at church, and I enjoyed the kids very much. One of the children made a suncatcher for me. It was a cute red tulip with green leaves, and when I got home, I licked the suction cup and stuck it in my bedroom window. The window was in the back of the house and faced only railroad tracks. The flower looked beautiful there.

Mom came in the next day, saw it, and scowled.

"You need to take that down," she said. "It's gaudy. I don't want anyone to see it."

I thought of my brother's advice—to just comply and avoid trouble—but that wasn't working for me.

"Who's going to see it," I asked snarkily, "the hobo on the railroad tracks? There's nothing behind us but woods and trains."

She didn't respond verbally but ripped the tulip off the window.

"Gaudy things do not go up in my house," she said, and she threw it on the floor.

It was game on. I picked up the flower and said, "You are being absolutely ridiculous." I stuck it back on the window. "It's my room, and nobody can see it," I said.

"No," she said, gritting her teeth, "it's my room and my house, and I can see it, and I don't like it."

I remember her lunging at me. I grappled back. Gripping one another, we stumbled into the mirrored dressing room and then into my closet with the built-in shoe racks that everyone thought were so cool and amazing. There I was in this luxurious setting, being attacked by my mother—and for the first time, I fought back.

I put my hands through her arms and pushed

them both outward. Then I pushed her away and said, "Don't you ever touch me again. No more."

She looked surprised and weakened. I'd been told my mom had bones that were broken at a very young age and they never healed. She stayed crooked the rest of her life. But I was done.

"I am moving out," I said. "You can keep the car, the insurance—all of it. You're not going to control me anymore."

HEALING AWAY FROM HOME

I had moved out before to attend college at Oral Roberts University in Tulsa, Oklahoma. Being away from home for long stretches of time, free from the daily threats of physical attack and psychological manipulation, I began to see and think clearly for the first time. At some point I realized I was becoming a healthier person. I didn't wake up fearful except about the outcomes of my test scores. I had to find God for myself more than ever and decide how I wanted to live. Nobody was over my shoulder telling me how to behave.

"This feels a whole lot different, and I like it," I thought.

My brother was at ORU as well, though we didn't overlap much socially. I knew nobody when I arrived, and I didn't feel particularly needy for friends. I was too busy exploring the novel feeling of personal freedom.

After one year I had this urge to move back to Richmond to consider if I wanted to return to ORU or take another path. I enrolled in classes at a local college there, moved back home, and began trying to find another place to live right away. The plan was to return to ORU in January if I hadn't made other plans.

I started attending our church again, and it meant more to me now. Though I was a pretty faithful person, my lifestyle still had some gaps in it. I didn't party, but I hung around people who did. I actually considered it incredibly amazing that I never did drugs or smoked or slept around, considering the heritage my mother and father had given to me. That said, I still liked being social, and one night I went with a couple of friends to a frat party near the local college campus. I was not a drinker, but I wanted to meet other people my age, and that night I met a guy named Troy Maxwell.

Troy was engaging, fun, and most definitely not saved. I don't think he knew one thing about the Bible or Jesus. But he was interesting to talk to, and he was definitely interested in me, though a relationship was the last thing I was looking for. I let him know I was in a place in my life where I had seen a lot of nightmare marriages and didn't want one of my own. I'd also had a high school boyfriend for a while, and that did not work out well. I was not interested in going down that path again, though plenty of guys wanted to date me—Troy chief among them.

Finally Troy said, "Hey, what are all the walls for? Why are you so adamant about us not being in a relationship?"

"Because you're not on fire for God," I blurted out.

"I don't even know what that means," he said truthfully. "Tell me. Maybe I could be. If you're asking me to go to church, I'll do that."

I had meant it to chase him away, but he got even more curious about this being "on fire for God," and he fulfilled his word by attending church with me. His first time there, his life dramatically changed. He raised his hand and gave his life to Jesus, and it was real.

Troy started going to church more than I did. He went even when I didn't. Then he started correcting my behaviors. "Why do you listen to that music? Why do you hang out with those people?" Then the clincher: "Why were you even at the party where I met you?"

Troy, by all evidence, was getting on fire for God, and I was amazed. For several months I simply sat back and watched his pursuit. His radical change had an effect on me, and things started to shift about my future.

Troy and I became very involved in the church's youth ministry as youth leaders. We basically treated it like a second job, even though the pastor of the church didn't believe in paying anybody. Around this time, I started noticing things about myself that weren't as whole as I wanted them to be, but I was always able to say, "I'm not as broken as that other person." I chose the worst examples around me, compared myself with them, and came out looking OK. In any case, there was no urgency to dive into the pain. Life was exciting; Troy was fun. We were becoming serious about each other and about God—so why go into the dark places? I just knew I wanted to serve God. I didn't know what that looked like or how to walk that out, but the desire was growing within me for a brand-new path.

One time I said with my own mouth, "I never want to be a pastor's wife." I'm not sure why it came out, except that I saw our pastor's wife take a lot of shots and get critiqued beyond measure. I knew that if it were me, I'd be quick to tell my critics what was what. That's just my personality. But I never wanted to be in her position. Volunteering for youth ministry was something I could control. Beyond that I only knew I increasingly wanted to be with Troy long term.

STAYING IN RICHMOND

Plans to return to ORU went away after I met Troy. Initially even my mom loved him. Then, as it became clear that Troy and I gained strength from each other and weren't going to be controlled, she seemed to turn on him.

"Why don't you like him?" I asked her. "What has he done to you?"

"I think he's faking this whole Christian thing," I remember her saying, and then she actually spoke these words: "I watched him eat a sandwich, and he didn't even pray over it."

I felt her dislike was deeper than that. Troy's family came from poverty. His dad was a full-blown alcoholic and had lost all their money. His mom was a flower child with a purple shag rug and a pot-smoking habit.

"Are we going to judge him based on his parents? Because I certainly wouldn't want him to judge me based on my parents," I challenged her.

But my sense was that Troy's family heritage presented an embarrassment to Mom's image, so she tried to put roadblocks in our relationship: "I forbid you to go out with him unless he follows you home in his car," she said. It was another way to manipulate and control because we lived forty-five minutes away from everything, and this meant a lot of additional driving for Troy. But he still did it, and our relationship grew.

When engagement entered the discussion, Mom made it clear she would have no part in our wedding. I was far from heartbroken.

"We don't need you to be part of our wedding," I told her confidently. "I would rather have a little wedding with cake and punch and live my own life than have you control things."

We got engaged Easter Sunday 1992. A couple of

months later Mom came back with her tail tucked between her legs and said she and my stepdad wanted to pay for the wedding. I couldn't understand why at the time, but I can only assume that it was her way of keeping up appearances. I suppose our getting married in a back room of a church messed up her high-society ambitions, and she couldn't bear that.

I was too naive to realize that letting them pay for it also gave them a sense of control over what happened that day. I'll never forget during the reception when the bandleader stepped to the mic and said, "I want to read a statement on behalf of Penny."

"What?" I thought. "I didn't write anything."

He continued, "Penny always had a dream of having a wedding where her father gave her away with one last dance. This is the song that Penny wanted."

"OK, this is ridiculous," I thought. My mother had created an image of some nonexistent relationship and was now playing it out publicly. But I was wise this time: I took my brother's previous advice and just went with it. My stepdad came out to the dance floor and took my hand, and we danced. Then he turned me over to Troy.

With that I was free of them. Troy and I had a new life in front of us. Whatever it looked like, it wouldn't look anything like my past.

Little did we realize that all the broken bones we were bringing into our marriage would need to be healed in the years to come.

CHAPTER 4

MARRYING BROKEN

I DON'T BELIEVE THERE are such things as "marriage problems." Whenever I say that, people tell me, "Oh yeah? I've got some!" But what they really have are unaddressed, unhealed individual problems that they brought into a relationship. We join up our dysfunctions like trains going in entirely wrong directions. On those trains are carloads of baggage. No matter how charmed your life has been, we all bring some baggage into a relationship. You might look at your baggage and say, "I've got Louis Vuitton baggage—I'm pretty fond of it," but even that high-priced, good-looking baggage is weighing you down.

Marriage is a hilarious collision of two seemingly perfect lives—until you wake up and go, "Wait a minute—someone else's stuff is in my house," or,

"Hold on—the toothpaste is being squeezed entirely improperly. This must change."

Troy and I waded through those basic lifestyle changes as everyone does. I wasn't allowed to use the clothes washer or dryer at my parents' house because they were fancy machines and Mom didn't want anybody touching them. As a result, when I got married, I didn't know how to do laundry, and by the way, I did not want to learn! It was news to me that you are supposed to separate wash loads by colors. Troy's background was totally different. He always had rolls of quarters so he could wash clothes in laundromats, which is what he grew up doing. He enjoyed washing and folding clothes, and he found it relaxing. That was one area where we blended pretty easily.

But every other area seemed to require a whole lot of work.

Prince Charming

I was just twenty and he was twenty-three when we tied the knot. Like a schoolgirl I expected my husband to be everything I didn't have growing up. I literally came into marriage thinking Troy would heal and restore the broken parts inside of me and somehow replace whatever I had lost in life up to that point. I never said this out loud, but in my mind he was going to play the part of my knight in shining armor, fulfilling my childhood dreams and giving me a white-picket-fence existence. I put so much pressure on my newly acquired Prince Charming that when he did something that didn't fit the fairy tale, I bit at him.

"You just talked rudely to me. Prince Charming did not talk to the princess rudely. You need to go back and read the fairy tale."

Little did I realize I was sabotaging our relationship and compromising my healing by insisting that healing come through my marriage. My solution to my broken bones was essentially, "Finally! Someone who has to love me forever. This is going to fix it all." Well, it didn't, because that isn't God's chosen method for healing anybody.

For his part Troy had a bunch of broken bones that needed to be set as well. Similar to my father, Troy's dad succumbed to alcoholism, racked up a number of DUIs, wasted all his money on the bottle, and even injured himself so badly while drunk that he could no longer work. I never had a conversation with Troy's dad when he was not drunk. He had flasks stashed here and there. You could smell it on his breath in the morning. His favorite destination was a bar, and he usually needed someone to drive him there since he had lost his driver's license.

Obviously neither Troy nor I grew up around people who were healthy in their walks with God. Both of us were trying to piece together who God is and what normal life looked like. No one had given us a template for healthy married living.

One time during an argument I blurted out a truth

I had never verbalized before: "You're not supposed to hurt my feelings! You're supposed to make everything better!" There it was, my unrealistic expectation in all its unvarnished glory.

Thankfully I had married someone wise enough to see what was going on. Troy sat me down one day and said, "I am a really great husband, but I'm a lousy Jesus. I will never be Jesus to you."

I began crying, "What are you talking about? I don't know what you're talking about!" I was mad at him because I thought he, as the head of our marriage, was equipped to fix everything wrong with me. But he wasn't.

"That hole in your heart is not Troy-sized; it's God-sized," he continued.

I would never have said I was putting Troy above Jesus, but I was. Getting married would not fix everything in one swoosh of a cosmic paintbrush. Rather, 1 Corinthians 7:28 says, "Those who marry will face many troubles in this life." That's the Bible! You can't erase it. It's in there. If you marry, get ready for trouble. Of course it also says that he who finds a wife finds a good thing (Prov. 18:22), and I take that to the relational bank every single day.

But my marriage was not going to heal my brokenness. If anything, it put a magnifying glass over it, revealing it in all its ugly splendor. I was beginning to learn that marriage is meant to help us grow in selflessness, not cover up and fix all our stuff.

I wasn't prepared for my pain to remain after the *I dos*.

SPLINTERS OF PAIN

When a man and a woman get married, they are suddenly close enough to touch each other's wounds all the time. Pain can—and often does—increase after the honeymoon period. I heard John Maxwell say some years ago that many people go through life with a splinter. If you take the splinter out right away when you're a kid (or whenever it happens), you're fine. You may forget that it even happened. But if you leave it in until you're forty, it gets nasty and infected. It hurts all the time. The pain makes you engage people wrongly. They shake your hand, and you jump back and say, "You just hurt me!"

They're like, "All I did was shake your hand."

The truth is, it did hurt you, but it shouldn't have, because you should have healed already. Many, many people walk through life with infected splinters, getting wounded over things that shouldn't be wounding them. They didn't get the spiritual tweezers out back when it happened, so they need greater intervention now.

As Troy and I pressed on in our marriage, I realized that the pain of great losses remained inside of me, and I didn't know how to process it. Stuffing it down and controlling it didn't work. Pretending it wasn't there didn't work. Worrying about it constantly didn't work. Troy wasn't able to make it go away. So what was the answer?

CHOOSING TO GRIEVE

It took about a decade for the answer to come. In the meantime, Troy and I left Richmond to start a church in Charlotte, North Carolina, with our three small children. So I was somewhat surprised when I had reached the ripe young age of thirty or so and God said to me one day, "I'm going to need to rebreak you." I immediately braced myself, wondering how bad this rebreak process would be. I was not sold on it by any means.

I knew by then that I had never fully grieved the loss of my childhood. I had done some work here and there, pulling weeds out of the garden of my heart. I had made progress in dealing with things such as bitterness over my loss of innocence and the lack of protection I had received. I had forgiven people and been liberated from anger and frustration toward them. Good things were growing in my heart. But God wanted to renovate my garden entirely. No more pulling weeds—the Lord was asking me to till the soil and plow things under. I had created a lifestyle of weed plucking. He was envisioning a complete makeover.

And it was my choice whether to let Him.

If you've ever tilled up a garden or a lawn, you know that what's under the surface comes to the top. That seemed dangerous to me, like Pandora's box: when you open it, you can't control what comes out or what goes on afterward. I wrestled with the choice, wondering, "Is it even worth it? Do I want to go there? What if so much anxiety or depression pours out that it overwhelms me and ruins my life?" I felt we were doing pretty well—I didn't want to endanger what we had.

Still, the Lord kept putting His finger on the bones I had that healed crooked. It reminded me of when He spoke with the woman at the well about her hurtful experiences. I could feel Him say to me, "You don't get to go any further until you deal with this." That actually made me mad.

"I don't smoke or cuss or drink," I fumed at Him. "I'm faithful to my husband. I'm copastoring a church and raising children. Why are You picking on me? In the scheme of things this is a tiny little internal issue. It's not bothering anyone. Why can't You leave it alone?"

I viewed my heart's garden as full of nice flower blossoms. Yes, there were bare spots, places where I had planted showy flowers to obscure the holes and patches I didn't want to acknowledge. I had learned to cope with those places, but now He was saying that coping wasn't thriving. His plan was better. His design for me went deeper and higher than what I had managed to create by planting nice-looking flowers.

But if God got hold of things and plowed my flowers

under, all those beautiful petals would get dirty and crushed. He was asking me to lay down my self-image, my life, to start over somehow. That felt hugely risky, but I had this sense that the Lord doesn't want us to bear flowers but fruit. Many Christians, like me, look at their lives thinking things are just so pretty. We have this flower mentality when God is all about our bearing fruit. There were areas of my life that were in full flower but needed to be plowed under so the garden would yield something that nourished others, not just impressed them.

I still wasn't happy about it, but how many of you know that you don't need to be happy about something to move forward? I'm exhibit A of that. So I said, "OK. Make the changes You want. I open the gate and let You into my garden to plow everything under or do whatever You want there. My pain of resisting You has become greater than the pain of anticipation and dread. Take my flowers. Grow fruit if You can. I'm ready to be healed."

THE REBREAKING BEGINS

Not everybody chooses to grant God permission to plow up their garden or reset their bones. All of us have accidental breaks, things that shouldn't have happened to us but did. When life broke us initially, it was accidental, or at least unexpected. We didn't see it coming. But with an intentional break, you anticipate the pain and agree to it. This is where most people opt out because they can. They didn't have a choice the first time, but now they do, and they would rather live crooked, bent, and broken than go through pain again. To have your bones reset means looking brokenness in the face and choosing to experience pain again.

When you dig below the surface to find the reason hurting people's pain persists, they often confess, "It's not that I didn't search for answers; it's that I didn't like the answers I got." They had conversations with God about plowing up their gardens, and they closed the gates on Him.

I admit it's not an easy thing to open up to plowing, to know that pain is coming as God digs up things you buried out of sight. You anticipate old feelings roaring back, the sense of being out of control, the harsh memories of betrayal and hatred and abuse. It's not uncertain; you know it's going to hurt when you get rebroken. It's not an accidental break; it's submitting yourself to pain.

But what else are you going to do, walk around with your nose out of joint, looking weird, acting weird, and not even breathing right? God has better plans for us than that.

Jesus never tells us to ignore what happened. I love that Jesus told us to speak to the mountain and tell it to be removed. He never pretended the mountain wasn't there. Some people think faith is pretending obstacles don't exist. Faith instead says the mountain is there and you speak to it anyway. The pain is there; we speak to it anyway. The hard memories are there. We face them squarely and speak to them anyway. Faith tackles things head-on. Healing only happens by faith in the healer. He teaches us to face the most insurmountable mountains in our emotional lives and say, "Be removed and cast into the sea."

I knew I couldn't pretend my bones had healed properly. My brokenness was on display. I was being inauthentic, and fake is one thing I can't handle in others or in myself. I had to live up to my own standard, quit pretending, and face it in faith.

I also had a healthy dread of going through life and not bearing fruit. Jesus specifically said that if we don't produce fruit, we are cut down. If we do produce fruit, we are pruned (Matt. 7:19; John 15:1–7). There's pain in both areas. I concluded I would rather experience the pain of pruning than the greater pain of being cut down.

I was saying yes to life—a life where I was actually bearing fruit and not just pretty flowers. There are no flowers of the Holy Spirit, but there is fruit of the Holy Spirit. I wanted fruit.

Fruit Versus Flowers

A lot of people chase after pretty flowers, but flowers come and go. God doesn't ask us to chase flowers; He asks us for fruit. Flowers look pretty and smell great but don't last long. They don't stand the test of time.

There's a difference between results and success. When Moses was in the desert and struck the rock for the second time, he got results. As a matter of fact, the water gushed out, not trickled, and millions of people had their thirst quenched. He achieved a bigger result than ever, but he wasn't successful. It was a flower. It was not what God had asked him to do. Success would have been his getting into the Promised Land.

People still do the same thing—they chase results when God wants us to chase the fruit that remains.

Remember when Jesus cursed the fig tree because it had no fruit (Matt. 21:18–19)? A fig tree is different from some other fruit trees. Figs generally flower and bear fruit first, and then the leaves come in. Many other trees produce leaves first, then flowers, and then fruit. Jesus saw from a ways off that there were leaves on the tree, so He was expecting fruit to be there. But when He got up close to the tree, He saw there was no fruit. The reason He cursed the tree wasn't that He was hangry. It wasn't Jesus in a bad mood. It was because the tree resembled what Israel had become. It was faking fruit. The Pharisees in Israel looked good from afar with their phylacteries and robes, but upon inspection there was no fruit. That's what Jesus was coming against—a religious system that had the appearance of fruit but actually only had leaves and flowers. He called the leaders whitewashed tombs

(Matt. 23:27). The outside looked pretty, but within were dead men's bones, just like the fig tree.

I have watched ministers fall because they chased the *pretty*. Flowers appear fast. They can bloom overnight. Fruit takes months to grow and ripen. It takes consistency, endurance, getting dirty—and waiting. Jesus never said, "Bear flowers." There are no such things as the flowers of the Holy Spirit. Christians often want that quick satisfaction, the appearance of success. Those are flowers, and flowers don't sustain you. Fruit does.

Pain Is Your Friend

So I opened the door to Him, cringed, and began to study what it looks like to sit with pain, to stop sidestepping it, and to allow myself to hurt. That, I realized, is the first step toward healing. Setting broken bones means facing tough stuff straight on and acknowledging it was real. It happened. It felt terrible. Ouch.

So many of us train ourselves that pain is bad. When you are little and you scrape your knees, your mom comes out and says, "Shh, here's a lollipop. Don't cry." If you think about it, it makes no sense. The kid just scraped her knee—let her cry for a moment! It hurts. But we don't like seeing others in pain because it makes our pain real again. That's why we shush them up and promise them ice cream cones.

The Holy Spirit is far more practical, and He gave us tears for a reason. They help us when we hurt.

People who refuse to process their pain—and disallow others' expressing pain—live with a secret compartment, a Pandora's box that is actually controlling their lives. The hurt is still there; it's just not expressed in the healthy, God-prescribed manner of grief. So it pops out in all sorts of other ways. They eat the pain away, drink the pain away, entertain it away, or drown it with sexual fantasies. Addictive behavior is never about drugs, sex, excessive food, alcohol, and so on. It's saying, "I'm feeling pain, and I don't know what to do with it, so this is my way of feeling numb for a while."

Westerners don't know how to sit with pain. We avoid, avoid, avoid. We deny that we were hurt or that it was a big deal. Avoidance can look like sudden outbursts of frustration or anger because we're bottled and throttled like a volcano. It can look like, "I just need a glass of wine, and I'll feel better." It can be, "If I can just have a sexual encounter with so-and-so..." It can even look like a life of endless distraction: do a load of laundry, clean the floor, care for someone else, take a vacation, work hard, play hard, and stay busy. People live that way, running from resetting their bones.

The Bible depicts many examples of people sitting with pain. Job is one great example. Jesus in the Garden of Gethsemane spent the night with His pain and was in such anguish that He sweat drops of blood. Only a few people in recorded history ever did that because of such intense anguish. Paul had a thorn in the flesh and pleaded for it to be removed, but God left the thorn and gave him sufficient grace instead. So many times, I don't want God's grace to be sufficient—I want that thing gone!

Many of us are on the operating table of life, and God wants to do a great work in us, but we keep climbing down while He's resetting the bones. He's saying, "I'm the great physician. I can take care of this." But we don't sign the consent form for the operation. No doctor operates without consent, so God lets us limp out the door.

Yes, the pain of resetting is real. If a plant could speak while it was being pruned, it would be screaming the whole time. So would a pot on a potter's wheel or gold going through a smelting process to clear out the dross. Dross is the impurities found in precious metals. You can't even see it until the gold is broken down. The only time dross comes out of gold is when gold melts and becomes liquefied. If you have never seen gold melting, it seems like it is being destroyed—but it's not. It's being purified in the only way possible.

When we are walking through things, we can feel as if we're being broken down, destroyed—but are we really, or is God up to something? God doesn't want your junky gold. He made you to be pure gold. He knows who you really are and that the dross in your life is not your true identity. He's got to heat things up to push that stuff out. He's after the real you. That's what resetting your bones is about—getting you living in your God-given identity as His pure and amazing son or daughter.

This is helpful pain we can choose. It is up to each one of us to choose which pain we will endure based on the outcome we want.

Pain is one of the best teachers you will ever have. It's not an enemy; it's an indicator. When people don't feel pain, they are dangerous to themselves and to others. There is such a condition, a type of leprosy, where people lack sensation. It causes them to damage themselves and never feel the injuries they inflict on themselves. What if you had a broken finger and never knew it? What if you had stomach cancer but nothing alerted you to it? Pain simply says, "Hey! Something needs investigation here."

Your pain isn't doing you harm; it's just telling you where the brokenness is.

ALL PAIN IS PAIN

Some people think that because they haven't experienced a big-time traumatic event in life, whatever pain they have is manageable. They believe they can ignore it, that it doesn't affect their lives, their relationships, or their effectiveness as parents, as bosses, as employees, as small-group leaders, or in whatever roles they play. But all unaddressed pain is damaging. The Bible says it's the little foxes that spoil the vine (Songs 2:15). In fact when you have little breaks that haven't healed properly, they can surprise you more than big things because you didn't remember they were there. Maybe envy creeps into your heart when a friend gets a nice new house. Maybe resentment takes hold when you compare someone else's marriage to your own. Relationships always bring out those little foxes. They expose vulnerable areas where we are weak, often because we healed wrong from some seemingly insignificant hurt.

The rich young ruler had everything together by all appearances. He was an up-and-coming leader, very wealthy, and young, and he had a seemingly great future ahead of him. But there was still an area God wanted to put His finger on. Like all of us, this man had a blind spot. It's so much easier to discover someone else's broken bones, especially when their breaks were dramatic. But as you go through life, you realize that small things have major consequences. Even a small fracture can debilitate you. If you break a pinkie toe, you will struggle to walk.

Jesus made this point when He compared anger to murder (Matt. 5:21–22). Few of us think that when we blow up at someone while driving, yell at someone at work, or speak angrily in our own homes, we are engaging in an activity on the same spectrum as murder! Yet the reality is that anger is far more damaging than it may appear. So is negativity, and so is complaining, one of Israel's gravest sins, which grieved God as much as anything else they did wrong.

Pain can hide in plain sight. One time I noticed that one of our young female employees was not speaking up in staff meetings. She was super creative, but I had to go to her after meetings to pull ideas and suggestions from her. Finally one day I asked her why she didn't speak up.

"I don't understand. What do you mean?" she said in response.

"You don't speak up," I repeated.

"I'm not sure what I'm supposed to say," she said.

"The same things you say to me when we're not in a staff meeting," I told her. "I want to know why you don't speak up when we're collaborating around a table."

"Because I was never allowed to," she said.

"What do you mean?" I asked.

"I grew up in a house where you didn't speak unless spoken to," she said. "My dad would tear me down and call me stupid when I talked, so I kept quiet."

Talk about hidden pain! This amazingly talented person didn't realize she had been broken in childhood and had healed improperly. As a result of this fracture she kept silent and robbed the world of her great ideas—probably costing herself a lot of positive responses, raises, and opportunities as well. It was a little fox spoiling her life.

People hide their pain by saying, "I'm shy," "I like to go with the flow," or, "I don't like to confront things." Those are signs of brokenness that didn't heal properly. We adapt to them and call them normal, but they always keep us from the full purposes of God in our lives.

It's time to ask the Lord to show us the little foxes, those subtle things we adapt to that are not pleasing to Him. We all have baggage; it's prideful to say we don't. Simply ask God, "What do my broken bones look like?" You may be surprised by what He points out.

SAFETY THROUGH STINK

Troy and I were getting ready to open a campus of our church in the Charlotte jail, and we met with the warden to ask what we should know.

"The majority of the prisoners do not take baths" was one thing he told us. "We have to force them to."

I assumed this was a safety issue, that they were afraid to be sexually abused. But he said that wasn't it. Rather, they were hurting so much on the inside that they didn't want anyone getting too close to them. Their smell repelled people and kept them at a distance. To put it in my words, they didn't want people jostling their broken bones.

People outside of jail behave that way too. I've seen it happen many times. They have angry outbursts, gain a lot of weight, or make themselves unattractive so their "stink" will keep people away. It's a way of rejecting others and avoiding the pain that might come with possibly being rejected. When you give people a reason to stay away, it doesn't hurt when they leave.

The Bible wisely teaches people to externalize their pain, their "stink," but only for a limited time. Those in Jewish culture who suffered loss had to wear sackcloth when mourning to acknowledge how they were feeling. People would know, "Hey, give that guy some grace. He is mourning right now." They put ashes on their heads, signifying death and decay. This was a great way to own how you felt—but it didn't go on forever. Today, when Orthodox Jews experience the loss of a loved one, they sit shiva, which means setting apart one entire week to mourn and feel every bit of the hurt. When they sit shiva, they grow their beards, tear their clothes, stay at home, and avoid reflective surfaces that would focus them on their external condition. They take every moment of that time to focus on the internal pain and mourn.

After a week they're done. This doesn't mean the hurt goes away. It just means they have fully acknowledged the pain and now they are heading in the direction of healing. What a healthy way of dealing with life's splinters, injuries, and losses.

Breaking Victimhood

As I sat with my pain, I began to realize how dangerous it is to live with broken bones. I could see that a mentality had been developing in me—a victim mentality. When you nurse pain forever, you subtly cultivate a personal identity as a victim. You weaken your character by emphasizing the lie of your powerlessness. You build up an arsenal of excuses that can be applied in any situation. You slough off responsibility, and somehow nothing is ever your fault.

Victimhood is perversely attractive because it takes a lot less energy to have a bad guy in your life whom you can stay mad at than it does to progress in personal maturity. It feels easier to hold a grudge than to grow up. Anybody—a man or a woman, a member of this race or that race, a rich man or a poor one—can convince himself that he is a victim. It absolves you of the responsibility of doing hard work to change. If I live my life saying, "I'm an oppressed woman living in a man's world," then I don't have to do the hard work of bearing fruit because my failure is always someone else's fault.

Victimhood is totally immature. I hate it. Yet in a backdoor kind of way I was becoming one.

The body of Christ has weaponized empathy and empowered victimhood, I noticed. We say we need to understand what this person or that person has gone through. We justify their inaction in the presence of broken bones. Isn't it time to tell people there's a healer? Isn't it time to explain that on the other side of pain is true hope and abundant life? How about we quit stroking their victim status and get them to face their mountains head-on by faith? How about we overcome some stuff?

The other thing a victim mentality does is blind you to your contribution to the problem. Yes, that's what I said. We all contribute in some way to the problems we have. Other people get to own what they did to you—no one made them abuse or reject you, and you certainly didn't invite them to. But you have to own the toxic thoughts you allowed to fester in your mind or your knee-jerk response to continue to blame everything on your childhood. That was you, not anyone else. Someone may have caused your pain, but if you're still feeling pain all these years later, you made a place for it to live.

It's uncomfortable to admit that part of the pain we feel when having our bones reset comes from accommodating the broken bones for too long.

HEALING STRONGER

Here's the great news in all this: even though it didn't feel good to have the Lord bring those hurts back to my mind so I could look at them and deal with them redemptively, I realized how kind He was to take me through this. I saw how weak I was with those broken bones unhealed. Resetting was making me stronger bit by bit. That's the great hope we have: He resets us to equip us for much greater victories.

One particular Bible story speaks powerfully to me about this. It's about a beloved Bible person named Jochebed.

What? You've never heard of Jochebed? Let's see if these details help you identify her.

Jochebed was in the middle of a traumatic situation. The ruler of her country was afraid that strong, hardy Jewish boys would grow up, band together, and topple his kingdom. So he decreed that all Jewish male babies must be killed. Jochebed was pregnant at the time. How would you feel if you received news that if you bear a baby boy, you have to let him die? Would you hide your pregnancy or maybe your baby? How long could that last? What would you do to avoid losing your infant son? This was a massively broken, hurtful situation, and Jochebed's emotions must have been all over the map.

But Jochebed went through the pain correctly. She put that baby in a little basket on a river, and he floated down to the palace, where he was rescued—the very palace of the Pharaoh on the very river where all the baby boys were supposed to have been drowned. The river that was supposed to destroy him took him to his destiny. God used that child to deliver the next generation from bondage. His name, of course, was Moses.

Here's my point: when you let God set your painful

circumstance in the correct way, He will release freedom to the generations that follow you. The river Moses floated down was dangerous. It separated him from his mother and could have taken his life. But that was the river that brought him to the palace, the place of training. He didn't go in the front door; he went in the back door. That's where we are headed. Your brokenness is a back door to the palace. It's the thing the enemy hoped to use to kill you, but it brings you to your place of destiny, even if you were expecting God to use the front door.

With Jochebed and with us, pressure is always present when there is a great promise. Your broken bones are meant to lead others to freedom. By letting God reset places of pain, you are going ahead of other people, clearing brush and rocks and stuff out of the way so they can follow more easily. Pioneers take people to new places. Pioneers are not perfect, untouched ones. They are scarred and healed ones. They are equipped to guide others to places of greater victory.

That's who you become when you say yes to the resetting of broken bones.

Biology tells us that physical bones always heal stronger. When you experience a break in a certain place, the bone fuses back denser and better, and you usually don't break there again. When we handle pain correctly, God equips us to go much further than we otherwise could have. We are like Moses, who emerged from his mother's pain to liberate an entire nation from darkness and slavery.

That is who you are. Your broken bone isn't just about you; it's about blazing trails and pioneering new territory for the people around you and those coming after you. It's about healing the nations. It's about the future of the planet.

CHAPTER 5

PANDORA'S BOX

A LOT OF STUFF came to the surface when I allowed God to start resetting my broken bones. Some of it I knew was there—and some of it I didn't.

FEAR OF ABANDONMENT

In the dirt right beneath my beautiful flowers was a fear of abandonment. In fact fear of abandonment *was* the dirt in some ways. Every person who was supposed to look out for me when I was young—my mom, dad, stepdad, grandparents, and others—either couldn't or wouldn't, so my experience told me, "You will always be abandoned by people who are supposed to love and care for you." That was my paradigm.

This view was on full display early in our marriage. Initially Troy and I both worked in the banking and investment industry. Troy carried a briefcase to and from work. When he got home and wasn't looking, I searched through his briefcase to see if there were any phone numbers or photographs of other women or if there was anything incriminating that would provide a gotcha moment for me. This was before cell phones, email, and digital photos. Nowadays someone would go through an email inbox, texts, or cell phone records.

Of course I never found anything because Troy was faithful to me. I just wasn't used to someone being faithful. I was used to being abandoned, and I expected it as a matter of course. Now the Lord called my attention to that mindset, and I saw how fear of abandonment shaped my expectations of other people's behavior. I was operating in the nonbiblical gift of suspicion, which poses as the gift of discernment but is actually a harmful counterfeit. The Lord called me out on it and taught me not to be suspicious of my husband, always looking for evidence of his wrongdoing. At some point you settle into a place of trust, with healthy relational habits and safeguards in place to uphold the trust.

In practice this mostly looked like telling myself that the suspicions that came to mind were false. I quit looking for evidence of bad behavior all the time. It took effort, but it began to work.

Fear of abandonment also surfaced whenever Troy and I got into an argument. I thought each fight would be our last. "This is it," I would tell myself. "It'll never be OK again. This is the end of our marriage." I could feel stress hormones released into my body along with those thoughts.

Of course arguing does not mean your marriage is ending. It was just my fearful mind rushing to the worst possibility—abandonment—that I could think of. I had to tell myself during arguments that Troy would not leave me, that this was not the end of our marriage, and that arguing did not ultimately mean rejection.

BREAKING EVIL FOREBODING

These were manifestations of a terrible mindset the Scripture calls "an evil foreboding." (See Proverbs 15:15.) In this frame of mind you wake up every single day anticipating that something bad will happen. For me, in my life up to that point, evil foreboding had often proved true. I had no problem believing for physical healing, which I witnessed in our family, or for financial provision, which happened for us all the time. But we didn't have a loving, caring environment where I felt fully safe to trust others. My experiences had conditioned me to believe that something bad was always around the corner and that it was unavoidable. Some people call it waiting for the other shoe to drop. I had heard many other shoes drop by the time I married Troy.

As I opened up to His touch, the Lord highlighted

places in my life where this evil foreboding was shaping my approach toward people and situations. I never would have verbalized it, but it was true. My actions were saying, "God, I really don't believe You are good. I'm not really trusting You." Even after ten years of marriage I would suddenly have the thought "Everybody's going to leave me. Troy's going to leave me. Everything's going to be taken from me." I knew this was probably rooted in my childhood experience of having good things given to me and then taken away to control my behavior. This interrupted my trust, kept my roots shallow, and made me wary of good people and good situations. It was an unhealthy expectation that evil would eventually control the situation—so I withheld my love.

At first I asked God to solve the evil foreboding by giving me more information. "Let me see the end of my story," I said in effect. "Then I'll come back to the chapter we're in and trust You." I wanted evidence of safety before giving my trust. But God does not work that way. The Bible says God's Word is a lamp to your feet (Ps. 119:105). If you have a lamp in your hand, you can only see a few steps ahead. Then you step into that and see the next steps. He doesn't give us headlights for our feet—He gives us a lamp that illuminates only the immediate area. That requires us to step where we know to step and trust Him for everything beyond that.

CHANGING MY INTERNAL DIALOGUE

Getting in tune with my internal dialogue was key. I trained myself to listen to the thoughts running through my head—and then I wrote down all toxic thoughts to expose them to the light. This became a very specific exercise for me, like hand-to-hand combat with evil foreboding. I literally started taking a toxic thought I had captured running through my mind and counteracting it by speaking or writing a specific truth from the Word of God. If the toxic thought "My future is uncertain, and I can't trust what God will do" came, I counteracted it by saying and writing down something like Jeremiah 29:11, which reads, "I know the plans I have for you." If I was wrestling with a lack of peace, then I found every Scripture on peace that I could. Maybe I had lost my joy. Joy is our strength, so I found Scriptures on joy. I did that with everything.

I had loved the Bible before this, but now I discovered new levels of power in speaking the Word of God. I had newfound faith in its ability to change my life. I thought I was doing well before, but close combat built skills and faith I'd not had before. It was amazing.

I saw how true it is that words are never neutral. When you say, "I'm so sick. I'm so broke. My marriage is a mess. I'm so depressed. I am so upset. I can't get out of this cycle. I never get a break," you are opening the door wide to those realities. Your mouth has creative power. It is the same kind of power God used to speak all creation into existence with the words "Let there be..." (e.g., Gen. 1:3). Proverbs 18:21 says death and life are in the power of our tongues. That is not just poetry; it's literal reality.

A great example of this is when John the Baptist was about to be born. An angel told his father, Zechariah, what was about to happen, but Zechariah spoke doubt into the situation. The angel shut Zechariah's mouth until the child was born, as if to say, "I am not going to let you use your mouth to destroy what God is going to do, so I have permission to shut your mouth until God's will is accomplished." Like Mama said, if you don't have anything good to say, don't say anything at all.

We have been given the power to speak life into our marriages, into bad relationships, and into negative health diagnoses. We don't ignore the existence of tough stuff. Before God spoke light into existence, the Bible plainly says the earth was dark and unformed (Gen. 1:2). Before Jesus raised His friend Lazarus from the grave, He plainly told His disciples, "Lazarus has fallen asleep; but I am going there to wake him up" (John 11:11). Don't pretend your broken bones aren't there. Call them out, and speak to them! This is why God gave you a tongue. Acknowledge the hurtful, difficult things, and then overcome them by speaking to them in agreement with the Holy Spirit. That's power.

In my own resetting, I took thoughts captive in a multitude of ways. One time I saw a picture online that looked like Jesus holding a little girl. It touched my heart, so I made it the wallpaper on my phone. When a negative seed floated into my thought life and tried to take root, I pulled out my phone and looked at the wallpaper to see Jesus with His arms around me in the form of that little girl. I said aloud, "Jesus loves me. Jesus has His arms around me." I wrote those words down or typed them into my phone. I visualized being held by Jesus as a little girl. Down in the dirt of my garden I worked with the Lord to change my thought patterns, a process the Bible calls renewing your mind. Instead of letting a bad seed grow, I uprooted it quickly. I preferred to pull something out as an acorn over as an oak tree.

God will give you multifaceted approaches when resetting your bones. The Bible refers to swords, spears, bows, and other weapons fitted for various battles. Become skilled in each one. Be like Nehemiah and build with one hand while holding a sword in the other. For my part I still put a sword through evil foreboding when I wake up each morning. I know how to defeat it in multiple ways. It is a daily habit for me to bring the fight to the enemy and subdue it before it comes against me. I am an overcomer in this area because I continue doing the work.

ALLOWING MYSELF TO BE LOVED

As a kid I had conversations with God and felt His concern and love for me. But I didn't have loving relationships with adults. More specifically I didn't know what it felt like to be loved for who I am. Later, when I grew up, my friends told me all the time that I seemed so confident and secure, and that is true to a point. I've never struggled with insecurity or needing people's approval. But I also didn't know how to receive love very well. When God started resetting my bones, I was surprised to find this one broken.

Evidence came in a few ways. When you're in the ministry, people often want to bless you by giving you something of value. Sometimes it's a small gift; sometimes it's something bigger. But anytime people tried to bless us personally, I always cringed, and I didn't know why. Troy doesn't have this issue, by the way. He's more like, "I grew up poor. I grew up eating government cheese. I have no problem receiving gifts." But I did, and it confused me.

Early on, before we moved to Charlotte, I owned a little red sports car. Because we were moving, our kids were really little, and I had made a financial commitment to our Richmond church that I wanted to fulfill before moving, I sold the sports car. That left me without wheels, which was a problem for us.

Troy and I prayed for three months, "God, Penny needs a car. We need You to show up big." One day I got a call from church friends who wanted to drop by for a quick visit. They drove up, walked in, set a little box on our kitchen counter, and said, "Don't open this until we leave." Then they left, and I opened the box. Inside were the keys to a Volvo station wagon that could fit all my kids. They had just given me a car.

I called them on the phone and said, "You can't do this. You can't give me a car."

Troy was standing there mouthing, "Are you crazy? You prayed for three months!"

But it was too much, too good of a blessing. These friends didn't back down but insisted I receive it, and they were right to do so. When I hung up, Troy demanded to know, "Why would you want to give it back? This is what you asked God for." He was so right. I knew I needed to learn to receive, because I couldn't even let God answer my prayers.

This happened again when Troy lost my wedding ring. It wasn't hugely valuable because we didn't have a lot of money when we got engaged, but we were getting ready to move and start a church, and now I had no ring.

A jeweler in Richmond whose three kids had come up through our youth ministry heard about the loss and said, "I want to take care of you. You've taken care of my kids for all these years." I reluctantly agreed, and one day he sent a courier over with a new ring. This one didn't require a magnifying glass to see. No way—this was a four-carat diamond ring you could spot from across a parking lot. I cried for weeks with gratitude.

But believe it or not, I tried to give that ring back to the jeweler who gave it to us. Troy shook his head and said, "You're a fool, woman." But to me the ring just seemed too big, too much to receive. Troy got after me again: "Did you not pray? Does it not say God will do exceedingly, abundantly above all we ask or think?" (See Ephesians 3:20.) I had to agree those words were in the Word of God. I just had a hard time letting them happen to me.

The simple truth was I hadn't been trained to receive love, so I automatically blocked people from blessing me. Perhaps I was rejecting their love before they rejected mine.

Interestingly I was also learning how foolish it was to let my own mother have an all-access pass to my heart, knowing she would hurt me nearly every time. Deep down I was still hoping she would show me unconditional love, but it never happened, and I was repeatedly hurt by her. Troy would get angry about it and call me out, saying, "You're trauma bonding. You need to cut that relationship off. It's completely unhealthy, but you've gotten used to the dysfunction. You don't let anyone else do that to you."

He was right, but it was so hard to accept that I would probably never experience love from my mother. I wanted to let her in even when the chances were slim.

One day, when I was struggling with forgiving my mom for what she did and didn't do after learning her father was abusing me, the Lord told me, "There's a difference between a wall and a gate."

I found this phrase interesting.

"A wall keeps everyone out," He explained. "A gate decides who can come in."

He was solving two of my relational problems at once. At the time, I was a wall with everyone but my mother. I kept people out and tried to reject their love but kept letting my mother in and getting burned. That was no way to live. In fact the Lord was saying that I was keeping Him out, even though I was only trying to keep pain out.

"I want to come in," He said.

Who could resist an offer like that?

So I began to use my relational gate. I opened it for people who wanted to love and bless me with kindness and friendship, and I trained myself to receive their love and blessing without fear. With my mother I became far more cautious and let the wall do its work, so I was protected from much unneeded pain.

Walls and gates—I wouldn't have learned this unless I signed the consent form to let the Lord reset my bones, one by one.

I began to see more clearly how much people need people. In fact I can't find one instance in Scripture where another person was not involved in someone's healing. We read of friends carrying friends to Jesus, a father pleading on behalf of his daughter, a mother interceding for her son, and so on. In the same way, the Bible says it's not good enough to confess our sins to God; we must confess them to one another (Jas. 5:16). Why? Because others need to be involved in your healing, whether that healing is physical or spiritual.

CALLING OUT MY FEELINGS

Self-awareness proved to be a huge thing for me through all of this. I tried to become really aware of what I was feeling and thinking, because I was learning in this resetting of my bones that feelings often lie. They seem like reality, but often they are not. They remind me of the Rebel Yell roller coaster at King's Dominion amusement park, where I would go as a kid. On that ride, one minute you're fine, and the next you're going up, down, and sideways and wanting to throw up. That's an accurate picture of our emotions. They go up, down, and sideways, suddenly change direction, and frighten us. Sometimes we just hold on, waiting for the ride to end.

When you are a kid in survival mode, you pick up necessary but ultimately unhealthy defensive habits. These help you protect yourself. But then you grow up, and the dangers disappear. The overly cautious stuff you did at age five to stay safe, you are now doing by choice as a thirty- or forty-something-year-old, and it gets in the way of life and genuine relationships. What used to be healthy is now causing you harm.

God is so kind to those of us who have been through bad stuff as kids. I realized He will protect us and be tender with us for a long time before calling us to move to a place of greater maturity. One of my favorite scriptural examples is when God led the Israelites out of Egypt—not by the shortest way, because they would have encountered enemies that were too scary for them to handle. The battle would have sent them scurrying back to Egypt. God knows what we can take and when it's too soon to begin active resetting.

But though He is tender, after we have been out of that hurtful situation long enough, God wants us to bear fruit. When survival turns to healing, we have to choose to open the gate to let God's love in.

TUNE THE ORCHESTRA

Troy has a saying: "Don't tune the orchestra after the band's already played." It means we should create solutions before problems appear. Identifying my thoughts is one way I tune the instrument *before* a concert, not after. I usually wake up and spend time reading. I make declarations over my thoughts, my family, my marriage, and my life situations. I don't wait until I encounter an issue or a bad situation. I tune that instrument right away so it sounds good throughout the day.

One thing I do regularly is pray for the people I can think of who hurt me. I don't want negative feelings toward them to shape my thoughts or behavior toward anyone else—that would be a discordant melody, so to speak—so I pray for them until I no longer feel pain when I think of them. It's hard to dislike or resent someone when you are praying, "God, pour blessings on that person and his or her family." Positive words crowd out negative thoughts. It's a fact. Your mind does not have room for both.

Tuning your instrument before the concert makes you a powerful, proactive person rather than a reactive, off-key person. Now let's look at the stuff that gets in the way of resetting bones—these barriers to healing that we must overcome.

CHAPTER 6

BARRIERS TO HEALING

B EHIND A LOT of unwillingness to change is standard-issue human pride. In our culture pride often looks like being a freethinker, an educated person, an independent voter, or someone who makes up his or her own mind on everything.

I have a little news for you: you don't have the right to be a freethinker. As a believer you have what Paul called a "mind controlled by the Spirit" (Rom. 8:6, CJB). You traded in your worldly thinking for God's higher thoughts. His opinion is the only one that counts.

Here's another uncomfortable truth: God often uses other people to correct you and me. I'm convinced that's why He created marriage. Your husband or wife will make you as mad as snot, but that's what relationships are for. People say, "I didn't hear from God about that issue," and I say, "Oh yes, you did.

From that person and that person and that person"—including your husband or wife. When we agree to let God reset our broken bones, sometimes we sit there waiting for lightning to flash from on high, when God has put the answer in the mouth of someone right next to us.

How do you know it's a message from God? It's often the one you don't want to hear.

PRIDE CAN'T HIDE

A couple we knew stopped getting invited to hangouts because their children were so over-the-top rowdy and out of control. These kids jumped on furniture, went upstairs when you told them not to, and displayed not a single iota of manners toward adults. It was really irritating to be around them, even though we all liked the parents.

The life group this family belonged to had stopped meeting for the summer, and I had a conversation with the group's leader about what they were going to do to address the problem.

"We're thinking one of two things," the leader told me. "Either start the life group up again and not tell the disruptive family, or we'll just cancel it altogether."

"You didn't talk about the third option," I said, "the one where you go to those parents and tell them their children are disrupting the group."

His eyes went wide at my suggestion. It grieves my heart when people keep moving on until they find friends who adapt to their kids. Real friendships are so rare that friendly correction is almost nonexistent. Everything remains nice and on the surface. We need more real relating.

"Are you kidding me?" he said. "You've been pastoring long enough to know that when you say anything about someone else's kids, you might as well put on boxing gloves—it's going to be a fight. Anyway, we don't want to hurt their feelings."

"That's not true," I told him. "Anytime you avoid something because you don't want to hurt someone's feelings, you're avoiding the pain you would feel from their response. You're not protecting their feelings—you're protecting yours. If you really cared for them, you wouldn't want them to be excluded because of this issue."

This hit pretty squarely, and I urged him, "You have an opportunity to win a brother and possibly keep this family in relationships they value. If you're really doing life together, and they won't hear you, it's not on you; it's on them."

This guy didn't like the idea, but he actually did it. He went and had a hard conversation with the father of that family, letting him know his children were behaving disrespectfully toward parents and houses. As expected, the kids' dad lit up the leader like the Fourth of July and the couple were indeed angry with everyone in the group for weeks. They felt their children were being disrespected—but that wasn't the leader's problem. He did his part in love and kept their group going.

Two weeks later the disruptive family apologized and asked for help with the children. They essentially said, "Wow, you guys are right. We need to do better. There are things that we have overlooked and need to deal with." The result was deeper relationships and real solutions because everyone humbled themselves to have difficult conversations—and one family didn't get offended by correction.

Are you willing to grow? Could you receive tough correction like that? If not, you're not in real community because in real community your feathers get ruffled. People rub each other the wrong way when they're in close proximity. That's how God intends it to be.

Correction, Not Condemnation

As local church shepherds, Troy and I have to correct people all the time. Our commission from God is to direct and guide people, which means turning them around when necessary. One of the main barriers we see to people's growth is that they experience correction as condemnation.

Troy and I were visiting and ministering at another church one time, and Troy picked up on little signals that the pastor's son was using drugs. Because Troy grew up in a household where drug use was normal, he sees the signs easily. While at dinner with this couple, Troy brought up the uncomfortable possibility of their son using drugs, and the pastor responded quickly, "No, not my son."

Obviously we could have set the topic aside and continued on, but we are determined to love our friends well, so we pushed the issue further.

"Listen, you don't have to believe what I'm saying, but there's a really simple way to find out," Troy said. "Go to CVS, get a drug test, and have your teenage son pee on it."

The couple looked at us aghast, but Troy said, "I've been around drug use for so many years that I can pick up on it. But you're the parents—it's your call."

Nobody wants to ruin relationships, but it wasn't about being right; it was about rescuing someone, waving the red flag so a kid's life could be saved. Dinner continued, and at least they didn't walk out on us then and there.

Later that night, the couple called us on the phone. They had done exactly what Troy suggested, bought a drug test, had their son pee on it, and watched it light up with everything from heroin to cocaine to marijuana. They were already planning to seek treatment for him.

Would that have happened if they had received correction as condemnation? They would not have discovered the truth that night and may not have in time to rescue their son.

A similar scenario happened a second time with

a different family in a different city, but instead of receiving the observation, they blew up at us and didn't want to speak to us again. A couple of months later it became public that their son was in a rehabilitation facility. He had overdosed on black tar heroin and collapsed in the mall. Medics had to pump his stomach to save his life. What if the parents had listened to the word of warning as the other couple had?

The lesson is pretty simple: if someone loves you and cares for you, listen to them! If you are in ministry or business or whatever, and you're so caught up that you don't see or accept the signs of danger in your own family, take a sabbatical. Come off the road. God is so good that He'll send a life raft to rescue your kids and your family, even if you missed the initial signs of danger.

I never want to be part of the band on the Titanic, playing like everything's good while the boat is sinking. I want to be the one hollering for people to get in the lifeboats so they can get to safety. This goes for big things, as in the examples earlier, and for daily things as well.

Recently Troy came to me late in the day after we'd had a, shall we say, corrective encounter about something we disagreed on. But instead of coming at me with an argument, he said, "You told me something earlier that made me want to pop back at you because you were correcting me. But you know what I did?

I checked that response and was really able to learn from what you said to me."

I said, "Boy, you look sexy when you talk like that!" Humility is the most attractive attitude around. Try it on sometime.

Jesus was always correcting people, but modern Christians too often sissify Jesus. They act like He went around only encouraging folks. The gospel was given to course-correct us, and that doesn't usually feel good. But when you can't receive correction without feeling condemned, you won't move forward. Your filter is off. Correction (through the wrong filter) looks like an enemy instead of a loving friend. "Faithful are the wounds of a friend," wrote the wisest man, Solomon (Prov. 27:6, NKJV). Friends don't stab you in the back; they stab you in the front! They don't gossip behind your back; they say it to your face. "Change this! Check yourself before you wreck yourself." That's course correction, not condemnation.

People who don't know how to receive correction don't know how to receive God's love, because Proverbs is very specific: God corrects those He loves (3:12). If you can't receive correction, you can't receive rescue.

When was the last time somebody corrected you and you responded, "Thank you for caring enough to bring that to my attention and not leaving me where I was"? Wow! That's true Christian maturity.

KEEPING US OFFENDED

The world around us thrives on stoking feelings of condemnation and offense. It is part of the enemy's plan to keep us from growing through loving correction. It keeps us from having our bones reset and healed. Think of how many billions of dollars the news media and social media make on people being offended. There's always something to be offended about, so people log in to get their daily dose of offense. They're shocked about this and mad about that, and the next day they sign in and come back for more. We feed our offenses because that's how we're conditioned to relate to the world.

The problem is we're not. God never made us to run on the fuel of offense. It will ruin your engine. The world will keep serving you offense as long as you keep buying it, but it neutralizes your strength, your focus, and your fight.

The plain fact is that nobody can offend you. You read that right. Nobody can offend you. Only you can decide if you are going to be offended. That's why Jesus said, "Blessed is he who is not offended because of Me" (Luke 7:23, NKJV). We make the choice to be blessed or to be offended. This happens throughout each day. We may witness a wrong or hear terrible news, but we don't have to let it offend us. We can call it out as wrong without letting it engage our emotions in the form of offense.

I like to joke that our church has six campuses instead of the five we actually have. The sixth, I say, is the place where all the offended people go when Freedom House's stand on this issue or that provokes them to leave. I like to imagine them meeting in some place together, feeding off each other's offenses. I think it's a funny picture—but also sadly accurate in many ways.

If your church isn't doing something that might offend you regularly, you are in a man-pleasing, overly accommodating place. Shepherds have crooks for a reason, and I'm not talking about criminal crooks. The shepherd's crook is meant to grab a sheep and pull it back from danger. It's to gently guide the sheep along the good path. We all need correction. The shepherd isn't there just to pet and praise us. Jesus said many things that caused people to quit following Him because they chose to be offended. What a personal tragedy for each one of them.

It's bad news for us too when we choose to be offended. When God reaches down to set your bones, it tests your ability to accept correction without experiencing condemnation or offense. God does not condemn us—therefore we are uncondemnable. God does not offend us—therefore we can be unoffendable. This is your calling as a healed person in Christ.

I grew up near a big DuPont chemical plant. DuPont created a substance called Teflon. It's the coating in a pan that makes it nonstick. It's a great picture of what we can be—Teflon Christians. Stuff slides right off. No offense sticks to you.

FORGETTING MY BIRTHDAY

One year Troy completely forgot my birthday. As someone who grew up pretty much neglected, all of my emotional baggage was sitting nearby like a crate of dynamite ready to explode. The whole day went by as I waited for some acknowledgment of what day it was—none came. Troy did his usual thing. I thought maybe he was planning something big and wanted to spring it on me. But he wasn't. As six o'clock rolled around, Troy had the gall to say to me, "You seem a little touchy today."

That was the only trigger I needed. I unloaded on him like a warship, using every bit of my ammo. "You know why I'm touchy? Because it's my birthday, and I have got nothing from you—not a kiss, not a card, not an 'I love you.' Nothing!"

Troy's expression said it all.

"Oh my gosh, I feel awful," he said. "Can I take you out to eat?"

"No, you can't take me out to eat!" I barked. I was in no mood to be wooed.

For two weeks I remained furious with him because I didn't think he understood the intensity of how he hurt me. I finally told him, "You got off way too easy. This was beyond 'I'm sorry.' When there's a deep cut, there needs to be deep surgery. I feel like you didn't do enough to fix it."

I got up the morning after that conversation, and there sat a birthday card on my nightstand—backdated to my birthday. I went downstairs, and there on the fridge was another birthday card. I got in my car, and a card dropped down from my visor. These weren't just cards saying, "I love you, babe." They said, "I realize how hurt you were. I'm sorry for the pain. I'm sorry for how I made you feel. I'm sorry I overlooked you on a day that you should have been recognized."

I went to work, and there was another card on my desk. I'm here to tell you, after all that, it was a lot easier to forgive and trust. Because when you bury something alive, it doesn't die. You have to dig it up and deal with it. For two weeks I was trying to bury it alive, and it wasn't working. Troy's grace toward me and his apologies helped pull me back to that unoffendable place. Truthfully it was a season of life when we were really busy. He was on the road a lot, and I could have let him off the hook more easily, taking into account the many directions his mind was going in. I shouldn't have taken offense as I did.

I got smarter too. I told his assistant, "Put my birthday on his calendar. Buy my present. Make sure he remembers." You can actually plan to avoid offense by doing practical things like that. I was learning.

TRUST THE PROCESS

In another painful season, Troy and I had a very difficult time getting pregnant. We prayed for years to have a child, but it wasn't happening. I wanted to be a mom so badly, and there were many heartbreaks, many pregnancy tests tossed in the trash.

One day I was crying about this, and Troy asked what was on my mind.

"It's just hard today to feel like I have lost that dream," I told him.

"Come here," he replied. "I want to show you something God spoke to me."

He took me over to his day planner—of course this was way before smartphones—and flipped back a few months to where he had written two words: "Baby, July."

"What does it mean?" I asked. I wanted to be sure because when my husband says God told him something, I take it to the bank. Troy almost never plays the God card, and when he does, his track record is phenomenal.

"God spoke to me, 'Baby, July,'" he said. "I'm telling you not to worry. Just trust God."

I started freaking out and crying because I knew God was good to His word, and I believed what Troy said. It was already May, and it seemed logical that I would be getting pregnant soon because July was just around the corner. I called all my friends to tell them,

"All these battles I've been fighting are coming to a victorious end. Troy got a word from God about it. July is coming! Pray with me. This is going to be the best year of my life."

I was amazed that my dream was about to happen. Then May came and went. Nothing happened. I began to think through every possibility. Did God mean I would get pregnant in July or that it would happen in June and I would find out in July? Either way I didn't care.

Then June came and went. Nothing changed. I figured God was making me hold on to faith for the promise that would happen in July. I bought a bunch of pregnancy tests and started using them on July 1. Every day, I took a test. One week went by. There were seven negative tests in the trash. Two weeks went by. Seven more wasted tests. Three weeks. Four weeks. Finally, July 31 came and went. Nothing except a trash can full of one-stripe results on the dang pee sticks. Now, to keep my hope, I had to change my logic.

"Aha! I've got it," I said. "God is waiting until the very last day of July for me to get pregnant, just to make sure I'm using my faith. I see what He's doing."

That meant the miracle would show up in August. I bought more pregnancy tests and used them daily. One week went by. Two weeks. Three weeks. Four weeks. The end of August came, and now I was so disappointed that I cried hard—so hard I got the "yicks." That's what I call those hiccup things when your breath comes in sharply. I had 'em—bad.

I marched in to have a conversation with Troy Maxwell, who was clearly a false prophet and the number one target on my hit list.

"How could you do this to me?" I demanded to know. "I was already fragile, and you smashed me into a million pieces. How dare you? You have never gotten something like this wrong—so why do you have to be wrong about this? You weren't prophesying, you were prophe-lying!"

Troy had no answer for me.

"I can't rationalize it," he said. "All I can say is what I heard: 'Baby, July.'"

"I don't believe anything you say anymore," I told him. "You heard wrong. You missed God, and now you hurt me."

You've had these kinds of conversations—I know it.

"All I know is what God said" was his only reply, and it sounded so weak to me.

I didn't get over it easily. October came, and I was supposed to go in for exploratory surgery to discover why I wasn't getting pregnant. At the time, I was working as a loan officer at a bank, so I divvied up my work in preparation of my absence. But the night before the procedure, I went into our den and could tell something was wrong with Troy. I did not like what he said.

"Babe, I can't shake this. I've been praying, and I

don't think you're supposed to have the surgery tomorrow," he told me. "I don't know why, but I just can't shake the feeling. I've wrestled with it. I've tried not to say anything, but the Lord has told me over and over again."

I snapped back, "I'm supposed to trust you? I've already made every plan to have this surgery. What in the world!"

"I'm just telling you that's what the Lord told me," he responded.

In the back of my head I was thinking, "Oh, I know; you're prophe-lying again." But because I trust the headship of my husband, the covering God put me under, I gritted my teeth and submitted to it.

"Fine. Fine," I said. "I'll call it off and show up to work, and they'll think I'm crazy, but they already think I'm crazy because I told them I was going to get pregnant in July. Thank you. I'll tell them, 'Troy said I'm not to have this surgery because God told him.'"

I told my boss I would be there the next day, and then I told the doctors I wasn't going to go through with the surgery because my husband didn't have peace about it. Of course my fellow employees were surprised to see me at work. They knew our struggle, and here I was canceling a good surgery based on my husband's opinion or gut feeling, whatever they wanted to call it. Honestly I wished Troy had never said anything about my getting pregnant.

Two weeks later I came down with the flu. It was

bad enough that I went to urgent care. After some tests the doctor came into my room.

"Mrs. Maxwell, you don't have the flu," he said. "You have a baby."

His words overwhelmed me, and I began sobbing. He continued, "We're really glad you didn't have that procedure because it would have aborted the baby. Your child will be born in July."

Wow.

I went home and told Troy that he was right—right about July, right about canceling the surgery. He said something that really stuck with me: "We should have trusted the process. God didn't say, 'Pregnant, July.' He said, 'Baby, July.'" I could have saved a bunch of money on pregnancy tests and an even bigger bunch of worry had I come to that conclusion quicker.

Had we not trusted the process and held onto the word, we literally could have aborted God's answer— our child—because the timing didn't look the way we wanted it to. I learned a profound lesson about letting miracles arrive the way God wants them to. This requires weathering rocky terrain and answer-less months. It means not grieving a misinterpreted word from God and not becoming offended in a time of waiting.

The fact is Troy and I had two babies in the month of July—on the same day, two years apart.

"Baby, July." God's word was doubly true.

CHAPTER 7

SETTING MINISTRY BONES

SOME PEOPLE THINK that going into full-time ministry will shield them from pain. If only! Not only did I have to learn to let God reset my broken bones in everyday life; I had to let Him reset the breaks that came in the realm of ministry, which is its own special kind of battleground.

I love the story of Paul and Silas, who in response to a dream from God journeyed to a rough town called Philippi. These guys were doing all the right things, and they got totally burned anyway. That is such the story of ministry.

It started with a little slave girl possessed by a demon who seemed to tell the future through dark inspiration. The name of the demon that possessed her is literally translated "a spirit of python,"[1] which is a chilling picture of the spirit that was at work through her. Paul and Silas did something righteous and compassionate: they cast that demon out of her. But suddenly she wasn't making money for her owners anymore by telling fortunes, and the owners got mad.

Fast-forward, and you see Paul and Silas dragged before city leaders, accused of wrongdoing, stripped of their clothing, and handed over to a violent mob to be beaten—at the encouragement of city leaders. Then they were imprisoned without having their wounds cleaned and placed in the darkest part of the prison with their feet in chains.

Ever felt like that?

You say, "God, I'm doing what You asked me to do in ministry, and people are coming after me. I'm being accused of things I didn't do, and now I'm getting beat up and imprisoned."

Some of us have shackle marks around our wrists and ankles, scabs and scars on our backs and shoulders, many of which came through obeying God in ministry. Every time we look at them, we wonder, "Why did that happen to me? It wasn't my fault. I was doing good, but still I got slammed."

I wish I were as holy as Paul and Silas were, so when I get beat up in ministry, I sing and pray at midnight. I'm just saying I need extra grace for that. Ministry will break your bones as much as or more than anything else.

But that's OK because God can reset them too.

Not OK Examples

As a young couple, Troy and I served in a church that we only realized later was severely dysfunctional. Everybody seemed messed up. The pastor's family was broken and chaotic. Staff members were sleeping together in broom closets. As weird as our own personal backgrounds were, Troy and I seemed downright normal compared with everyone else because we had left our pasts behind.

One time we were in the church's green room, and there was a big-deal, big-city pastor talking about the affair he'd recently had. This man had just come off the platform, where he had given an altar call and led many people to the Lord. Now he was saying rather casually how he didn't consider his dalliance to be an affair because he and the woman didn't "go all the way." He talked about how the woman sat on the front row and cheered him on. He lamented that his wife wasn't more affectionate.

Troy and I sat there in shock. Our pastors told us, "This doesn't go out of this room."

My husband and I looked at each other like, "This is not OK."

Troy also traveled occasionally with another man, a minister he highly respected for his anointing and spiritual gifting, which were very real. But back at the hotels Troy saw women come and go from this married man's room. One time this man confided to

Troy, "I envy what you've got." He meant a committed, steady relationship like we had, though we had been married just four or five years by that point. This man's marriage was predictably falling apart.

We also witnessed what you might call spiritual abuse, which I define as twisting Scripture to justify bad personal behavior. The pastor would say things such as, "Your ministry comes before your marriage or your kids because God gave Adam a garden before He gave him Eve or children." That didn't sit right with us. I thought of the Scripture that says if you don't care for your family, you're worse than an unbeliever (1 Tim. 5:8). The Bible says to judge things by their fruit (Matt. 7:16–20), and the more we looked, the more we didn't like the fruit we saw in the lives of leaders in this church.

I am not complaining, and I am not embittered. I am grateful for what God did in our lives during that season. But I am also being clear-eyed. The Lord let us see bad stuff early so we would not repeat it when we started Freedom House Church. It was like being inoculated against habits that could have consumed us.

INVESTIGATOR

Still, because people in positions of authority had hurt and abused me when I was little, I went into ministry expecting a level of loyalty that no one could possibly give. My unspoken attitude was, "Don't ever hurt me, betray me, or lie to me." These conditions were unattainable, yet I put these unrealistic expectations on people.

As I mentioned before, I can easily turn into an investigator if I don't trust somebody. I become hypervigilant. All my senses get switched on because of what I perceive as a potential threat. But as I said, there is a difference between the discerning of spirits and suspicion. One is a gift; the other is the after-effect of trauma. Some people go around sniffing out other people's sins and secrets—at least according to their imaginations—but really they are reacting to a persistent fear of being ambushed because they were hurt in the past. Now their "gift" supposedly protects them and others from potential bad guys. They are always waiting for something negative to be revealed so they can say, "I knew it! I told you so. I warned everyone."

It is evil foreboding wrapped up in shepherd's clothing, and when I saw it operating in my life, I knew it needed to change.

I had to figure out how to lower my expectation of people and raise my expectation of God. Sometimes we do it the other way around. We place a huge expectation on people, and when they disappoint us, we don't know how to respond. Many people then make it God's fault. It never is.

My initial proposal to God when Troy and I started the church went like this: "I've seen what happens to people in ministry. They have bull's-eyes on their backs, and they get harassed and targeted by people. I'll go into the ministry on one condition: guarantee that I won't get hurt. Then I will do everything You ask of me."

God responded and said, "I'll counteroffer you. You will get hurt, but when you do, I'll be there." That's how I began to shift and learn to trust God. That's also when He gave me the analogy: "No matter how hot the heat gets, don't let anything stick to you"—just like Teflon.

In some ways I think I overcorrected on that lesson, and now I'm pretty much everybody's best friend until they stab me in the back. I don't wait to warm up to people. I go all in from the beginning—until and unless they get weird. There probably is a better place to be, somewhere in the middle, but I prefer to be open and friendly rather than distant and suspicious.

I also understand that sometimes I hurt people and am the imperfect one in the relationship. Some time ago someone in our church made an unkind post on social media about pastors. I assumed he was making a dig at Troy and me, and we'd had some other issues with this guy. I called to ask him about the post, and it turned out it wasn't aimed at us at all. I apologized for my suspicion and accusation.

We all come with as-is tags on us, and I'm that way too. We have to be willing to accept other people's frailties and forgive each other readily.

BUZZARDS IN THE SANCTUARY

Though I don't operate in the fake gift of suspicion, I can pretty easily spot people who may not be healthy to hang around. The warning signs seem to me like buzzards flying over their heads. What are buzzards drawn to? Stink and rotting meat.

One sign of a buzzard is when someone says, "I love this church. It's so much better than the last five churches we've attended." That's a sure sign of something rotten. I'm definitely sniffing something and seeing a buzzard circling over that person.

When people don't have appropriate boundaries, I start sniffing something and seeing the buzzards. Recently a woman who had attended our church for two months kept private-messaging me on social media—on my day off—about her personal need. I let her know the church's team could handle her need, but she kept pushing me to get involved. "I want to get together and tell you everything," she wrote. When people push you, it's because they think they can. I politely let her know that she was coming up against boundaries I set. I barely knew her, it was my day off, and her personal problem was not mine to solve.

When she continued to push and complain that our team didn't respond to her yet, I got firmer: "I'm sorry the team hasn't contacted you yet, but I have boundaries in my life for a reason. One is a day off. If I don't have one day to bring my thoughts down, I'm no good for everyone else. Also, if I tell you someone else will take care of it, that's how it is."

I could see a whole flock of buzzards circling over her head by now, and I wasn't going to stick around to find out what the stink was.

Another sign of buzzards is the way husbands and wives treat each other. When the husband says, "Everything's great. We're doing so well," I look at the wife's countenance because it cannot lie. What does her face say when he says that? Does she withdraw into herself? Or are her eyes agreeing with his words?

There are other signs as well. How do people treat their children? Their waitresses? The janitor? Most people put themselves in a specific spot on my mental map within five minutes of talking with them. Out of the abundance of the heart the mouth speaks. They reveal who they are and if there is anything to be wary about.

I don't go buzzard hunting when I meet people. Rather, I love people and welcome them into my life, but when I see buzzards flying over someone's head, I am more than OK with keeping my distance. There is an important balance between remaining open and guarding your heart. I don't need unnecessary broken bones, and neither do you. I want to set myself apart from those who could hinder my healing. The Bible says some people bring fire into their bosom and get burned (Prov. 6:27). That means they bring the wrong people too close. You don't need that self-inflicted harm in your life.

This is especially true if you are actively dealing with past hurts under the counsel of the Holy Spirit. Recognize when you are vulnerable. Guard your heart. Jesus one time called the father of a dead girl away from his family members and dearest friends so their doubt would not touch his faith. If people are laughing at or mocking your solution, do what Jesus did: "he put them all out" (Mark 5:40). There are times to put people out of your life, sometimes temporarily, sometimes forever. Protect the place where your miracle is happening.

Protect the place where God is resetting your bones.

YOUR PEDESTAL WON'T HELP ANYONE

Another snag I faced in ministry was this false idea that only I could solve people's problems. Because of my background I was the one who went after the hard cases, the people who'd gone through the worst stuff. I was the one bringing the stray dog into the home, only to realize that wounded dogs bite.

In the early days of ministry I thought, "If we are there for everyone, they will all be healed." Because I felt neglected and abandoned as a child, I had a high standard for not neglecting or abandoning someone else. I drove myself to be available to everyone 24/7. I thought I could give them what they needed to be healed. I was putting myself in a category with God. It was a trap.

My attitude was rooted not in guilt but in pride. Somehow I was more important than God. Only I could provide the solution. I would drop everything, call a babysitter, and go save someone's marriage. I thought I was loving people that way.

Monday is Troy's and my only day off, and it seemed we always got marriage crisis calls then. I would leave what we were doing to dash off and help whoever needed help. I felt energized and useful, but I was neglecting my own marriage on our only day to decompress and reconnect. I justified it by saying things like, "What if they get divorced if I'm not there for them?"

Then one day the Lord confronted me, saying, "Oh, so you're the one? If you don't go, their marriage is over?" I had to take a closer look at what I was doing and why. I began to see that that kind of thinking would cost me dearly.

We used to get phone calls at 3:00 a.m. for all kinds of pastoral emergencies. Then people contacted us on social media saying things such as, "I need money today, and if I don't get it, my kids and I will be on the street. My lights will get shut off." Each of these things was a huge boundary buster we had to learn to deal with correctly. I felt like saying, "You and your husband are fighting in the middle of the night, and you're waking up me and my small children, demanding our help and wanting an answer in fifteen minutes to a problem you've spent fifteen years creating?"

I learned the wisdom of that old saying about not letting someone else's crisis create an emergency for you.

It's not healthy or helpful for anyone when we try to play God. There's a difference between caring for someone and carrying someone. So many people want your prayer time and the blisters on your knees and your intimacy with God—so they don't have to earn their own. I read somewhere, "God wants intimacy with us, but He isn't an easy score. He expects marriage and covenant, not one night stands."[2] People want a quick fix, but He wants a love relationship.

I have found that people who want me to do the work don't prosper in the long term. We can't allow their flattery of us to turn us into their fishmongers so we feel important, like their providers who keep giving them fish. The best thing is teach them to be fishermen. Some people have been saved so long that you have to part the whiskers to insert the bottle. If you have facial hair, you need to be eating meat, not milk. It's time to do the work on your own.

To see if somebody's hungry for real answers, I often give them a book recommendation. "Get this book, and let me know when you're done reading it," I say. They almost never do it, and this weeds out people who want me to be their god versus those who are hungry for the one true God. I'm willing to help most anyone, but if they aren't willing to work on their issues, neither am I. I've spent so long working on my stuff that I'm not willing to be in close relationship with people who aren't willing to do their hard work. We aren't in Old Testament times anymore, where people need an intermediary to communicate with God. No, our job as pastors, friends, and loved ones is to help them hear God's voice for themselves.

Our best counsel and advice will never take the place of the answer God wants to give them in the context of a real relationship with Him.

LET THEM GO OUT THE BACK DOOR

This may sound gross, but the Bible compares the church to a body. When you look at a human body, it has a back door where stuff exits, and we flush it away. Things that don't need to be in our bodies anymore leave. A church body functions in the same kind of way.

At first it felt like a personal loss to me whenever someone left our church. But there is a natural cycle in church bodies just as in our physical bodies. In my earthy analogy, think of it as your church having healthy, regular bowel movements. When people exit your life, your church, or your business, it is often God's protection. It's normal. In fact you can tell a lot about a church by *who* is leaving. It's natural for some people to leave and others to join, and occa-sionally you have to clean house, or in this case clean the pipes. You don't want chronic diarrhea, but some-times things need to be emptied out.

I had to learn that holding on to people or things that were not meant to be in my life was actually harmful. Now, instead of feeling loss and pain when any relationship adjusts itself, I accept God's guidance and timing for that person as he or she exits my life.

I don't "flush" anyone, but I learned to let people go out the back door.

MAN-OF-GOD SYNDROME

One of the bone breakers in ministry is what you might call the man-of-God syndrome. Ministry can attract people who love crowds rather than people. They want the focus, the adulation, the spotlight. I've seen some change as they step into the pulpit. They grab the mic a certain way, tip their pinkie, and say, "Ha!" as they walk across the stage. They know how to look at the camera in a certain way at the right time. It becomes a performance.

One minister actually told me, "You wouldn't like me when I'm not preaching."

"Why?" I asked.

"Because when I'm preaching, I'm under the anointing," he said.

I thought, "You mean you're only anointed on the

platform? You're different everywhere else? What kind of consistency is that?"

We must be impressed by fruit, not flowers. Fruit indicates multiplication, legacy, and sustenance. Gifts don't dazzle me anymore. I look for someone who is the same on the platform as in person. I look for shepherds who have the smell of sheep on their clothing. I watch how men and women of God treat people who can't do anything for them.

I look for those who don't isolate themselves in a green room all the time. I understand there are crazies and people who gobble up your time, but that's a tiny percentage and shouldn't keep you from everyone else. As leaders we must teach people to have boundaries, not to adapt to their dysfunction. We learn to say, "I have to speak in a few minutes, so I have to go. Why don't you contact our office, and someone will be glad to talk to you?"

Leaders should be among people, not apart from them.

We need to kill celebrity culture. At Freedom House we call our raised front area a platform, not a stage, because a stage is for performance; a platform is for influence. Signs on our doors declare, "This is not a stage; it is a platform. Thank You, God, for using me." Every person who goes on the platform sees that: band members, ushers, and speakers. Everyone knows it is an honor never to be taken for granted.

Celebrities tend to burn out. They burn brightly

and then fade. I don't want to be a shooting star but a North Star. I don't want to fade out. I want to stand strong and be a light to help others navigate toward Christ for a long time.

BLACK-DIAMOND SLOPES

Troy and the kids were skiing a few years ago and made a wrong turn to a much more difficult slope. Looking down over the edge, they saw a field of moguls that could have proved dangerous. That was just not going to work. Somehow they found their way over to an easier run, and that saved their day.

It's the same in life. Head down the wrong slope, and you start thinking, "How did we get here? This stuff's killing me. How do we get back on the right slope?" This is a snapshot of boundaries that are so important in life and especially important in ministry. Don't put yourself in situations that cause broken bones. If you belong on the bunny slope, stay on the bunny slope. Don't test the black-diamond slope.

When Troy and I were youth pastors, I taught the teens, "How do you keep yourself out of trouble? Don't put yourself in situations that could lead to something bad. Don't get halfway down the slippery slide at the water park and say, 'I want to go back up.' It's too late. You shouldn't have climbed the steps and jumped onto that slide in the first place."

One of the boundaries in our marriage is that no

man gets in my car alone with me, except Troy or my son. One day a male employee and I were heading across our nearly thirty-acre campus at the same time.

"Hey, can I hop in the car with you and ride to the next building?" he asked me.

The trip would have lasted thirty seconds, but I still said, "Nope. You can ride on the hood if you want."

He thought I was joking, but I set him straight.

"My husband and I have a boundary," I said.

"For real?" he inquired.

"For real," I affirmed. "Once you've been married for thirty years, you can talk to me about it. Until then, you can get on the hood."

So he did, and I drove him across the parking lot.

One time a couple made an appointment to see Troy for counseling during the evening. But that night, only the wife showed up to our church building.

"Where's your husband?" Troy asked through the glass door.

"He can't make it. He had to work late," she said.

Troy didn't even open the glass door.

"I can't talk to you," he said. "We'll have to reschedule. I'm not going to counsel a woman here at night by myself."

She was not too happy, but Troy explained, "I've been married since 1992, and I aim to keep it that way."

ANTI-FAKE

On the other hand, Troy and I welcome into our lives people whom others might reject. For example, a new family came to church one time. I was speaking that day, and they were sitting toward the front. After the service they came up to me and said, "We want you to know, the only reason we stayed is because we were sitting toward the front and didn't want to walk out in front of everybody. We don't believe women should be preaching."

I replied, "Hey, that's great. A bunch of us are going out for pizza across the street. There's a great pizza shop there. Wanna come?"

They looked at me like I hadn't heard them properly.

"We just insulted you, and you're inviting us to pizza?" they asked.

"Sure," I said. "I don't mind. I don't need your approval."

Bewildered, they came, and I bought their pizza. For two hours we talked about the Bible. I said, "Whether you come back or not, I'm glad you came, and I hope you continue to dig into the Word."

They had warmed up substantially by this time.

"Actually we liked what you said," they said. "It's just that you're a woman. But you're not offended by us?"

"Why would I be offended when God called and equipped me?" I asked. "Why would I think twice about what you say?"

Believe it or not, they showed up the next weekend.

"What are ya'll doing here?" I asked, not meaning to sound so surprised. Then they came back a third week and alerted us, "We will be on vacation next weekend and won't be at church."

Not long after that the campus they were attending had a woman speaking, and I wrote to them beforehand, "Ha ha. Giving you a heads-up that a woman is speaking there this weekend."

After church that day, they came up to our executive pastor and said, "We want to join this church." This family's three boys had told their parents, "Mom, Dad, she's awesome. We like her."

Why did we accept these folks so readily? They crossed none of our boundaries. They were ignorant but not weird, pushy, or predatory. They just needed to be taught the Word of God. I'll walk a thousand miles with sincere people but not with people who cross boundaries.

MESSY BUT REAL

There was a guy recently who didn't realize Facebook was checking him in everywhere he went. It checked him into a strip club one Saturday night and checked him into our church the next morning. As people saw this on his feed, they began to light him up with harsh comments—but I loved the way he responded. He said, "My life is still messy, and I'd rather go to a church that doesn't reject me when I blow it." Then he posted a picture of the empty seat next to him at Freedom House that morning and invited people to come to church!

Is it OK to go to strip clubs? No! Those are abused, trafficked women—but that man was also entrapped by lust he couldn't control. There are losers on both sides of that equation. Would I rather he stayed home from church after he messed up? No way. I want him getting better, not worse.

One guy came into church one Sunday and afterward said, "That was the best [expletive] message I ever heard." It was just part of his vernacular. I told Troy, "I'll take him over someone who comes here and acts perfectly, then goes home and uses that language." Bring your mess, but don't bring your hypocrisy.

Etched into Troy's and my personalities is that we can't be fake. I have a visceral reaction to fakeness. Fake is counter to who we are. It rubs us completely wrong when we see people putting on an act. We have worked on this extensively in our own church, and it helps that Troy and I are open about our pasts and our failings. I much prefer broken and real people to fake ones. I'd rather someone cuss me out truthfully than pretend to be my friend and talk behind my back. If you're real, I'm good with that. We can make that work.

Those are some of the ways we avoid broken bones in ministry and also allow God to reset them when breaks happen. I took God's counteroffer, and He's been good to His word every time.

CHAPTER 8

LIFE HACKS

W<small>HEN</small> I <small>BECAME</small> a Christian, I didn't understand that I was signing up for battle and enlisting in the army of God. I didn't see the part in beautiful Psalm 23 where it says He prepares a table for me in the presence of my enemies (v. 5). Or the part that says even though I'm a sheep following the Good Shepherd, I'm going to walk through a valley of death (v. 4).

It took me a while to figure out that as God's kids we are placed into a theater of war. He expects us to fight—and to win.

A DEMON ON HER SHOULDER

One of my more unusual spiritual-battle experiences took place when Freedom House was just two years old and meeting in a school auditorium. We were between services, and I looked out and saw a woman who caught my attention. I knew something wasn't right with her, so I walked over to her. As I approached, I visibly saw something dark on her left shoulder and realized it was a demon. A couple of thoughts went through my mind, the first being: "How did that thing get into church with her?"

As I approached this woman, the creature leaned over and whispered in her ear. It was crazy to watch.

"Are you OK?" I asked her.

"No, actually I'm not," she said. "I keep hearing voices in my head telling me to take my life, that I'm not worth anything."

I said, "Do you realize there is literally a demon on your left shoulder, whispering in your ear?"

"That's where I keep hearing it," she said, "on the left side of my head."

"I will pray with you, but you must agree with me because it will want to come back and bring more," I told her. "Do you want this gone?"

"Yes, I do!" she said and began crying. We prayed and that thing literally jumped off of her shoulder and ran out the door. My honest thought was, "Why didn't it just go through the wall? The door was further away." I found it all very interesting, to say the least.

The woman then said, "I am really ticked off right now. I thought it was my own voice, that I was down on myself about my own life. Now that I realize the devil had an assignment against me, I'm mad! I'm never going to let him talk to me again."

That was some hand-to-hand spiritual battle and a good reminder that things may look one way in the natural, but there's a whole spiritual component at play that we often cannot see. The problems with your finances, your kids, or your marriage are not taking place entirely in the natural.

The problem is that Christians get whooped up one side and down the other because we don't know how God fights. We have weapons but don't know how to use them.

A Raccoon and a Gun

The Christian life requires that we use the right weapons to fight our battles. Sometimes the battle is spiritual and the primary weapon is prayer. Other times the battle is in the realm of our habits and the primary weapon is discipline. Most battles require a mix of weapons and approaches to skillfully overcome the problem.

When Troy and I were first married, we got a puppy, a little toy poodle. I was in the habit of getting up once or twice a night to potty train this dog, and about that time, in the middle of the night, I began hearing little footsteps on the deck outside our bedroom. I told Troy, "There's someone on our deck," but he would dismiss it and roll over with, "Everything's fine. Just go back to sleep."

But after four or five days, I knew I wasn't making it up, so at 4:00 the next morning, the thumping came onto our deck, and I woke up Troy.

"Go check it out!" I insisted.

He went to the sliding door and opened the curtains and the door, and there before him was a raccoon the size of a small child. This thing wasn't afraid of him at all, and it was pretty clear he had sniffed out the puppy inside our house and was hoping to find an easy way in. He waddled off into the night, and Troy came back to bed.

"We need to call pest control to bring one of those big cages out so they can capture and relocate him," I told Troy, but he had a different idea.

"Don't worry your pretty little head over it," he told me. "I'll take care of it."

"What does that mean, 'I'll take care of it'?" I asked.

"Babe, I've got it," he told me. "Don't even worry about it."

This was the point where if I had been a more seasoned wife, I would have investigated what exactly he had in mind. But as a new wife still finding the boundaries of our relationship, I relented and said, "Fine. You take care of it."

It wasn't twenty-four hours later that we were sound asleep when our little masked visitor made himself known on the balcony. Troy leaped up, slid the door open, and saw the raccoon.

"What are you doing?" I asked him.

"I'm just making sure," he said. Then he went to his dresser, opened the top drawer, and pulled out a gun.

"What is that?" I demanded to know.

"It's just a pellet gun," he said nonchalantly.

"A pellet gun?" I asked, staring at this thing in his hand, which looked like much more than a pellet gun.

"A pellet gun," he repeated, as if a woman wouldn't fully understand guns unless they were patiently explained to her.

He marched toward the door with that "pellet gun" in his hand, slid the door open, and rapidly let off four shots. The problem was it didn't sound like that gun was shooting pellets. These were the loudest booms I had ever heard up close. Troy proudly came back to bed, apparently having warned the creature off our deck.

"Troy, that's going to wake up the whole neighborhood! And the next neighborhood," I said. "What are you thinking?"

"Nah, it won't," he said, coolly lying back down.

By this time, I was figuring out my boundaries real good, and I knew this man needed help understanding the situation.

"Troy, we need to call the police and tell them it was you who did that so nobody will be worried," I said.

"Nobody heard that," he said. "It's four o'clock in the morning. They'll think someone's car was backfiring or something."

"No," I said, "they're going to think someone shot off a gun."

"Just go back to sleep," he said. "Don't worry about it."

It was no surprise to me when, not long after that, blue and red swirling lights filled our room.

"I told you," I said. "You need to go outside and deal with this."

I scurried out to the front door and stood behind it in my pajamas. Manfully Troy went outside where I could hear him talking to the officer.

"I'm sorry, officer. It was me," Troy said. "I was scaring off a raccoon with a pellet gun. I didn't mean to wake anybody."

"A pellet gun?" the officer said.

"Yes," said Troy with undiminished confidence.

"I need to see your pellet gun," the officer asked.

"Yes, sir," said Troy and came inside to fetch it. He brought it outside, and the officer examined it.

"Sir, this is no pellet gun—it's a .22 caliber pistol," the officer said. "Do you realize there were people out watering their flowers, and they heard you fire this and thought someone was trying to murder them? They dropped to the ground, army crawled back toward their house, and called 911 to investigate. Do you realize what you've done?"

"I'm really sorry," Troy continued. "It's not even registered to me. A friend let me borrow it." Then he added, "Why did I just tell you that?" realizing he had just tattled on himself.

Thankfully the officer was more interested in other things.

"Sir, are you married?" he asked.

"Yes, and my wife told me it was a bad idea," Troy said. "I shouldn't have done it."

"Sir, where's your wife?"

"She's inside," Troy replied.

"Would you go get her for me?" the officer said.

"She's in her pajamas; she won't want to come out," Troy protested.

"Sir, I need to visually lay eyes on your wife," the officer said firmly.

That's when I was summoned onto the porch, in my pajamas, to wave at the officer and all the neighbors who had gathered to see what was going on.

"Hi, officer, we're newly married, and he hasn't learned to listen yet," I said.

"Ma'am, are you OK?" the officer asked me.

"Yes, I'm OK," I replied.

"Do you feel threatened in any way?" he asked.

"No, I do not. We're fine," I said, then added to the neighbors, "I'm so sorry, everyone."

That was the last time I let Troy take care of a wild animal. Wrong weapon, wrong result.

BASIC WEAPONRY

The Christian life requires detailed familiarity with a basic set of weapons, such as prayer, worship, Bible reading, fellowship, obedience to God's commands, financial generosity, hospitality, fasting, and more. There are plenty of really good resources on these things, but I want to zero in on some that helped establish a culture of healing and wholeness in my life, marriage, and church. They pertain to letting God reset our broken bones.

The first thing is knowing the difference between insulation and isolation. One is healthy; the other is dangerous.

When people, leaders in particular, walk through heavy stuff, they are tempted to say, "I'll walk through this alone—just me and Jesus." They isolate themselves because they are afraid their masks will slip. Ministries, churches, businesses, and most organizations put leaders on pedestals and turn them into heroes. The problem is heroes always fall from their pedestals. Nobody belongs up there.

An expectation of perfection pushes leaders to draw back and cover up. In the Bible Israel's first king, Saul, isolated himself because of insecurity. Even when he was anointed king, he hid behind his baggage. All of us have baggage in our lives, things we're not proud of. Saul came from the tribe of Benjamin, which was known for an ugly incident involving rape and a brutal murder that led to the decimation of the tribe. Saul was ashamed of his past, so he wondered why he was to be king, saying, "Am I not a Benjaminite, from the least of the tribes of Israel?" (1 Sam 9:21, ESV). He was still dealing with past insecurities. He thought people would say, "Hey, Saul's a Benjaminite. Remember the terrible stuff they did."

Saul's life went on to demonstrate that instead of overcoming insecurity, he isolated himself and accepted no help from godly counselors and friends.

Moses had a much better approach. He would get revelations from God on the top of the mountain alone, but he never lived on that mountain. He came back down to where the people were. Elijah and David got in trouble when they isolated themselves but remained healthy when they insulated themselves within healthy communities.

Jesus modeled this practice perfectly. If anyone could have rocked the just-me-and-God approach, it would have been Him. He was in perfect harmony with the Father. Many times He went out by Himself and was alone with the Father for hours. But as a man Jesus still needed human support. Even He didn't get the option of going through life alone.

In fact Jesus had to live within a community that was really imperfect, and this is a great point for leaders to hear. We often avoid relationships because we think they won't help things in the end; they can't change the outcome. But is that the point? It can't be, because Jesus stayed in fellowship with guys who frequently let Him down. The night before His death Jesus prayed all night and asked His friends, "Can you guys stay with Me? I really need you right now." He just needed some buddies to sit with Him. He knew it wouldn't change the outcome, but the fellowship was still important enough that He went back to them three times for the human connection.

That's very different from someone who isolates himself, pulls away, and becomes toxic, unhealthy, and unteachable. Proverbs tells us that a man who isolates himself breaks out against all sound wisdom (18:1). We aren't allowed to go through things alone. Isolation sets you up to get picked off by the enemy, the way that shoulder-perched demon was trying to take out that woman. Insulation within a healthy community sets you apart to grow.

THE RISK OF RELATIONSHIP

One of the greatest pictures of insulation versus isolation is in the account of the guys who brought their paralyzed friend to Jesus one day. You remember that these friends carried him on a mat to the house where Jesus was, but they couldn't find a way in, so they dug through the roof and lowered him down through it! As a result the paralyzed man was healed, and he carried his own mat back home.

Everybody in this account had very good reasons not to do what they did. Each took on significant risks.

Start with the paralyzed man. He was fully depen-
dent on his friends. For a lot of us that's an uncomfortable position to be in. We prefer to be the helper,
not the one being helped. This guy humbly allowed
himself to be toted around town like luggage in the
hope that he would get healed.

Not to mention that this was dangerous—really
dangerous. He could have fallen to the ground at
any point if one of the guys tripped or dropped part
of the mat. He could have been crushed by people's
legs in the crowd. Compare this to the relationships
you're in. Sometimes others are carrying us, and
they don't always do a good job of it. The disciples
"dropped" Jesus when they kept falling asleep in His
greatest hour of relational need. When you're being
carried, you could be dropped too. This causes some
to shrink back from the risk of relationship. Nobody
wants the pain of hitting the ground when people
fail us. But this guy knew he would never get healed
without taking this risk. We all need people to help
get us where we're going at times.

His risk was greatly magnified when the buddies
couldn't find a way in and instead decided to lower
him through a roof! It's one thing to drop someone
from ground level, and another to drop someone
from ceiling level. He was already paralyzed, but this
could have made his life much worse and possibly
killed him. This was not a cute Sunday school story;
it was a potentially fatal endeavor.

For their part his friends took on great inconvenience by taking him somewhere he couldn't get on his own. They carried a body, which is hard to do. They didn't give up but persevered through major obstacles: a thick crowd, a thick roof. Surface friends would have said, "Sorry, man. We tried. We couldn't get you near Jesus." The guy on the mat would've given them a pass and said, "Thanks, guys. You did the best you could." But that's not what happened.

The guys lugged this dead weight to the roof, then disassembled the roof, and then cooperated effectively to lower a man through the opening. None of this was easy, but they were legit friends who did not give up. They were not going to take no for an answer. And an answer is exactly what they got. Imagine walking home with the friend you spent all day carrying around on a mat. Imagine telling the story over and over to friends and family members and strangers. Imagine the incredible emotions and gratitude that would erupt everywhere. All of that happened because they took the risk of having relationship.

What miracle will you receive because of the help of friends? Do you have people in your life who will contend with you for these kinds of miracles?

GET A TEAM

One of the decisions that will determine the power and effectiveness in your life is who you surround yourself with. When Troy and I went into full-time ministry, we embraced the principle that "in the multitude of counselors there is safety" (Prov. 11:14, NKJV). Up to that time we didn't have many accountability relationships. We looked around and saw so many people going off track. They didn't have the kind of friends who called them on stuff, the kind who know you and "no" you. A lot of accountability happens organically with the friends you happen to have. They weigh in and say, "You shouldn't be talking to that old flame on social media. You shouldn't be staying out late when your husband or wife is out of town."

But Troy and I wanted a firmer foundation. A lot of people don't finish well. We wanted to. We wanted mentors who told us what we did and didn't want to hear. We wanted people who pushed us to check ourselves before we wrecked ourselves.

I also believe firmly in the wise maxim that the higher up the tree a monkey climbs, the more of its ugly butt you see. If you're in a visible position in the community, your mentoring accountability needs to be more formal. The taller the skyscraper, the deeper the foundation that has to be dug. Those who are more visible make better targets for the enemy. If he can strike the shepherd, he can harm a lot of sheep. When terrorists look for targets, they don't look for one-bedroom homes. They look for tall buildings and go after them with a wrecking ball.

This goes for fathers and mothers as much as

anybody. If anybody is looking at your example, you are a leader to that person. Everybody needs accountability. It's not just for those in visible or public positions.

So Troy and I created an internal board and an external board for our church. The internal board deals with the normal things a church board handles, while the external board deals with Troy and me and gets into the nitty-gritty of our personal lives to make sure we're healthy. They ask questions like: How do you spend your money? How frequently do you have sex? How fulfilled are you in your lives and ministry? Where are the trouble spots?

At first when they asked probing questions, I was like, "Hey, we love you guys, but why are you getting so personal?"

They said that leaders usually fail in three areas: glitter, gold, and girls. "In those three areas, we're going to get all into your life," they promised us. And they have.

We chose these external board members based on what we saw in their lives. They had long track records of stability and good fruit. They weren't shooting stars but North Stars. All are older than we are, and they happen to be in different cities, like Atlanta, Dallas, and Tulsa. They all know each other. Sometimes we're on a call all together for annual board meetings, but the majority of the time we're with them one at a time. Each has a different set of gifts and brings different perspectives and expertise to the task.

MARRIAGE COACH

In addition to this Troy and I made the choice to have regular marriage counseling as a preventative measure. In life you can either be in constant repair mode or constant prepare mode. Vitamins are preventative. I'd rather take them daily than repair damage later. I think every person and every couple should be in counseling, no matter who you are.

We think of our marriage counselor as a coach. You don't just go to the gym when you're overweight and out of breath. You go when you're healthy and fit. You don't go to the gym because you're weak; you go because you're strong and want to stay strong. A coach is someone you enlist to help you get stronger. He makes sure you're doing things the right way so you don't hurt yourself. He wants you not to lift more than you should, squat wrong, or run too much. He knows when you can do more in a certain area and says, "You've got five more in you. Keep going." With a good coach you do more reps than you thought you could, lift bigger weights than you thought you could lift, and do it all with proper form.

Troy and I do some counseling individually and some together. If we have a particularly difficult season and are frustrated with each other, we do more separately so the counseling doesn't turn into strife sessions that don't produce fruit in the moment. The majority of our counseling is done online because the particular counselor we work with doesn't happen to live in our city. We don't just talk to our counselor-coach when we're having a rough time. We talk when nothing's wrong at all to build up strength for whatever may come down the line.

We tend to stay with the same counselor for a long time because we like someone to know our story and our background, but we also like to seek additional help in areas where we are hungry for specific expertise. For example, we might seek a businessperson's counsel for business questions or use an executive coach for professional and staffing questions. We believe you should have people in all areas of life helping you go to the next level.

Of course this is all about accountability, not commanding. The decisions remain ours, and sometimes we disagree with our external board or other coaches. For example, there was a time when the economy was really bad, and we bought a new car to replace our eighteen-year-old vehicle. We jokingly said our old car was anointed because each week we had to put in a quart of oil. We loved that old thing, but it needed to go. One friend wouldn't even let us park it in her driveway because it dripped so much oil.

We bought an SUV, which was the best fit for our lifestyle at the time. We had three small children and were a mobile church, setting up and tearing down every weekend. On Sundays we packed the SUV full of stuff. But one of the people on our external board didn't like that we had bought an SUV when the economy was so horrible and gas prices were so high. He felt we should have gone for a car with better gas mileage. Troy and I had considered the wisdom of buying an SUV because of gas prices, but at the time, SUVs were very cheap and we took a gamble that gas prices would ease back down.

"That wasn't wisdom," this board member said, but we disagreed and thought it was. It wasn't a spiritual or moral issue, so there was room for disagreement. We had already bought the car with our own money, and we reminded him we had three children and a mobile church. An economy car wasn't going to serve us well.

A year later gas prices leveled out, and we actually had equity in the car. This board member told us, "You guys were right. I shouldn't have come down so hard on you about that."

Accountability is not there to rule you but to give you insight you may not have had. We appreciated his saying what he said, both his initial opinion and his later change.

A Board of Directors for Your Dating Life

I actually suggest getting a board of directors for any area of your life you feel could use extra wisdom or input. For example, a lot of people could use a board for their dating lives. These people tell you when your picker gets off, call you on your bad calls, and help you keep a kingdom purpose in mind. They enforce your rules and boundaries when you've gone off the reservation.

I say dating in particular because I've never seen people leave dating relationships better than when they went in. They go from one person to the next, having almost a series of mini divorces. It wears them down, the hurts pile up, their baggage gets full, and their bones get broken. The right friends, counselors, or board members can help prevent unnecessary breaks.

Some people come crying and tell me, "I don't know how my boyfriend and I got into this situation."

I say, "Let me help you understand: if you go to his apartment late at night, and he's got romantic music on and the lights down low—there is no mystery why you're falling into sin. Do you know it's really hard to have sex with someone when you're not alone together? Don't be together at his house at night alone. That's how babies get made."

Some women don't realize they are dressing for the wrong kind of success. Their outfits draw to them the kind of guy who thinks they are signaling that they're easy. I tell women if there are always sharks circling, maybe there's blood in the water. Maybe these guys are looking for an easy meal, so to speak. A good dating-life board member will ask you, Is the perfect guy you want to marry going to be drawn to the kind of pictures you post on social media? Boy, did it get quiet in this book right now.

I prefer courtship, which is based on dignity, respect, and honor. *Courtship* even sounds kingly and regal. Dating is a poor counterfeit for courtship in my view. Dating produces lots of broken bones.

BODY AND SOUL

I also have people who are allowed to speak into my physical health. Some women draw the line here and are not willing to accept any accountability in this area. But I think it's extremely important and has a strong spiritual basis. God Himself is a three-part being: Father, Son, and Holy Spirit. Humans are three-part beings as well: body, soul, and spirit. We were made in God's image. We are spirits, we live in bodies, and we have souls (which are our minds, wills, and emotions).

Why then would it be OK to ignore one aspect of who you are? It's like looking at one part of the Trinity and saying, "Jesus doesn't matter," or, "The Holy Spirit doesn't matter."

One time, a very large woman came in to talk to me. I sympathize with anyone who has wrestled with weight issues because like every woman, I have too. I told her, "You need to check and see what's off here with your physical situation."

"I just need to pray and read my Bible more," she responded.

"Nope, that's not all you need to do," I said. "Look at all three parts of you. You are not just a spirit but a body and a soul. God did not make your body to be obese and out of balance. You need to treat all three parts and find out why your soul is crying out so loud and causing these harmful physical habits."

Usually food addictions or imbalances aren't just gluttony but the manifestation of a broken bone needing to be reset. That's a problem in the soul that is crying out for healing. No diet can repair a broken bone. When we are unsettled, we reach for something to settle us. I've known many times in life when I just wanted to spend time with my good friends Ben and Jerry. They were always just a freezer away. But when I did and my physical health started changing, it never solved the actual problem.

One time, our external board members actually brought it up with Troy and me. I remember the phone call clearly. This accountability mentor and his wife had known me most of my life. He said, "Penny, your weight has jumped up. What's going on?" Most people wouldn't have touched that issue with a long-distance laser beam, but he went right there. He had always known me as a thin person who didn't struggle in this area, even though there had been a struggle there at some point. His wife was also on the call with us.

He started the conversation by asking Troy, "Do you still find your wife attractive?" He explained that he had seen issues arise in many ministry marriages over the years based on loss of attraction.

Troy answered, "I find my wife beautiful."

I was happy to hear that, but the man pressed in anyway and said, "I don't want you to have issues with your sex life," and he then asked me about my weight.

I could have easily fired back, "I've had three kids. How dare you!" I could have manipulated my way out of that accountability by making him the bad guy because the question and the whole topic hurt so badly in the moment. It was not an easy conversation. I did have three kids but in some ways I had let myself go. I had to acknowledge it and ask myself, What was going on?

Because of that accountability moment I went to the doctor and found out that there were some problem areas in my body that I wouldn't have known about otherwise. I had PCOS, polycystic ovary syndrome, which sends blood sugars out of balance and causes stress eating. The doctor put me on medication, and in the first week I lost fifteen pounds.

I then joined a running club for a brief time, and that got me moving again and helped me break through mental barriers. I also studied food groups and how my body responded to those.

The reason I discovered these things about myself and progressed in the needed areas was because this man cared enough to have an awkward and hurtful conversation with me. I have learned that hurtful conversations are not harmful conversations. Good hurt is when a dentist removes a rotten tooth. Bad hurt is when you leave the rotten tooth there because it's too uncomfortable to have it removed. To submit to accountability means hearing feedback that hurts— but helps reset that broken area. I would much rather have the pain and accountability of addressing a physical problem early than be talking about why Troy didn't find me attractive anymore.

Two years after that moment, another pastor who also had this man as his mentor came through Charlotte and said, "I need to talk to you guys. I'm really upset." We had him over and he told us that this same man had confronted his wife about her weight, which had gone up drastically, and its potential effect on their marriage.

The mentor also brought up the fact that their family woke up very late every day, they tended to arrive late wherever they went, and his wife was always promoting products to friends in a series of multilevel-marketing businesses.

Because the mentor went after signs that seemed to signal deeper issues, this man got angry and cut him completely out of his life. After he left, Troy and I looked at each other and said, "Everything that mentor brought up is just what we've been thinking about that family."

A couple of years later the wife had an affair, the family fell apart, the couple got divorced, and the church they oversaw was harmed. I looked at Troy and said, "I wonder if he had listened to counsel if things would have been different."

There are practical things we can do to prevent broken bones, and perhaps the biggest one is to be part of an accountable community with people you trust and listen to their counsel. It doesn't mean you always have to agree with it, but remember that you chose them to be in your life for a reason.

One reason may have been to spare you some broken bones.

CHAPTER 9

KEEP ON BLESSING

TROY AND I had our first child, Colby, when I was twenty-five years old. The years of struggling to get pregnant were over, and it was time to celebrate our new little family.

One day when Colby was still a little boy, my mother called.

"Penny, the family is getting together for Easter," she said. "Can you come?"

My response was immediate: "Why would I bring my child around a convicted sex offender who never even acknowledged publicly what he had done?"

The memory of her response still flabbergasts me. "Come on, Penny," she said, "we all know it wasn't little boys he was interested in."

In other words, she seemed to be saying Colby was safe from my grandfather's grasp in a way I had not been—and somehow this made it better. All I could think was, "Since when did demons become predictable? Nobody is safe around this man." The pain of that remark was awful but representative of our relationship. This was before I had learned how to have functioning gates and walls with my mother.

Of course Troy and I refused to go to the Easter gathering, and so did my brother and his family. Not long after that I was on the other side of town and happened to stop at a grocery store I never really shopped at to pick up a few things. There I ran into a relative I hadn't seen in a long time. She looked at me strangely as we began talking.

"I debated about calling you," she said. "I wanted you to know what happened at Easter."

Inwardly I went, "Oh no."

"The family all got together," she said. "We were in the kitchen when we heard a horrible noise in the den. We ran into the other room, and there was Gramps with his belt off, wrapped around my son's neck. The boy was passed out on the floor, unconscious."

My jaw about fell open.

"When we demanded to know what in the world was going on, he said, 'I don't know. We were playing a game,'" she said. "Then your mother yelled, 'You guys make sure Troy and Penny don't find out about this.'"

Picture the scene. An unconscious boy with a belt around his neck, my grandfather standing next to him, and it seems my mom was more concerned that Troy and I not know we were right about this predator.

The boy, she said, came to consciousness and was fine, aside from the mental scars from whatever had happened to him, which they didn't find out. Gramps died some years later, and I didn't go to the funeral. I had forgiven him and reconciled with what he had done to me, but there was no relationship there, and I would not honor an unrepentant child molester, even in death.

But you can bet I never once regretted keeping my children from the danger I knew he embodied. I spared them those broken bones I had suffered.

Rushing Back

With good walls and boundaries around us, life seemed really good. Troy and I had two daughters, and God blessed us as a family in so many ways.

When Colby was in middle school, he joined a church league basketball team, and my daughters became cheerleaders for his team. I was overjoyed to see my kids doing something so fun together. As a mother I was on cloud nine. The night before the first game I carefully packed their sandwiches, bought 100 percent juices and little organic snacks, and put them neatly in resealable gallon bags. On Saturday morning I was beyond excited. At the gymnasium I set their juices on the bleacher for each one of them, right next to their snacks. The game started, and I cheered on

Colby as he went up and down the court. My daughters jumped and shouted and cheered. Colby had told me, "Every time I make a basket, it's for you. When I pat my chest, it means, 'I love you.'"

During the game he shot a basket, turned to find me, and patted his chest. I just melted. "I don't care about anything else," I thought. "No beach vacation or awesome ministry assignment could match this. I would rather be right here on this bench, cheering on my children, than anywhere else in the world."

Then it happened. Without warning, my face was flooded with tears. I was uncontrollably crying on the bleachers of this church gymnasium. The thoughts went through my head: "If I feel that way about my kids, why did my parents never come to my games? Why did they not protect me when I was sexually abused as a child? Why did they side with my grandfather when he was sentenced to prison for what he did? If I love my children this much, why didn't they love me?"

In a horrible instant this great experience with my kids flipped to a different script. I felt the abandonment I had suffered all over again. Questions bombarded my mind: "What kind of parent wouldn't be there for his or her child? What parent wouldn't step in and protect a child from abuse? What kind of parent would be drunk all the time?"

That was when I really understood that each of us has to manage our forgiveness for a lifetime. It's not a one-and-done thing but a decision we keep on making. As we make it, it gets stronger, but it never completely goes away.

There had been times—a thousand, maybe a million—that I felt my anger was justified. My logic was excellent, my conclusions bulletproof, how it was right for me to feel the way I felt about what had been done to me. But my anger made me the proud owner of a white elephant. Let me explain.

Maybe you've participated in white elephant gift exchanges. There's a story behind that term. It is said to have come from a punishment given by the King of Siam to enemies he wanted to saddle with an unusable "gift." A white elephant was exceedingly rare, and there were rules for how one could be used—and not used. For example, it was illegal to use it for work. Essentially you could not use it for anything profitable. While a white elephant was purportedly priceless because of its rarity, the recipient of this large, living gift soon realized that he owned something that seemed to promise a great deal of value but which actually cost a lot to feed and house. Elephants live a long time, so this was the gift that kept on giving—or rather, taking.

Bitterness is like a white elephant. It offers a perceived payoff that turns out to be a trap because it costs you instead. When you continue to hold a grudge, it's usually because you perceive it to possess value it actually does not have. All the while you're caring for this useless elephant and spending energy to feed it, house it, and clean up after it.

Following are ten reasons I've observed that people (including myself) can hold on to unforgiveness:

1. Unforgiveness makes us feel strong. Forgiveness makes us feel weak. Forgiveness makes my pride bow its knee.

2. Unforgiveness allows me to control and manipulate others by making them feel bad about what they did. I hold it over their heads. This puts me in the driver's seat of the relationship.

3. Unforgiveness seems to protect me. What if you hurt me again? I don't like feeling vulnerable. I would rather feel angry because at least anger feels powerful. Unforgiveness keeps people at arm's length so they can't get close enough to hurt me.

4. If I ignore the problem, it will just go away.

5. Unforgiveness activates revenge. The other person has to pay and learn a lesson for what he or she has done.

6. I don't understand God's love and forgiveness, so I cannot extend it to someone else.

7. I have not forgiven myself. If I keep beating myself up, how can I let you off the hook? I treat others the way I treat myself.

8. Forgiveness seems too easy and unfair, like I am condoning sin. One time I got into an argument with Troy, and he quickly said he was sorry. "No, you're not!" I countered. "That was too easy." I wanted him to grovel and suffer more, though never once has God done that to me.

9. The one who hurt me has to come to me first. That person did the wrong. I didn't do anything. I'll sit here and wait for the person to knock on my door.

10. I am waiting to feel like forgiving. I don't have the goose bumps or love thing happening yet.

Those are all perceived payoffs. When you struggle with unforgiveness, it helps to figure out what your perceived payoff is and shine a big spotlight on it, exposing it for what it really is—a white elephant.

YUKON

One time I noticed a sloshing noise in my car while I was driving. Every time I turned left or right—sploosh! This water noise emanated from the back. I looked around, and there were no bottles of water rolling around the footwells. So I took the car to the dealership and asked why it sounded like I was driving a boat.

"Mrs. Maxwell," the mechanic told me, "your back left door is full of water."

"Full of water?" I said. "I didn't know that was a thing. I've never heard of it happening before."

"Yes," he continued, "and as a matter of fact the water level was almost high enough to submerge some electrical components, which would have shorted out the electricity in your whole car."

"This is news to me," I said. "How on earth did water get in my door?"

"A helicopter," he said plainly.

"A helicopter?" I asked.

"A helicopter," he said again. I thought he was referring to a type of car part that I was unfamiliar with, so I asked for an explanation.

"Here, let me show you one," he said and produced one of those little twirly things that maple trees drop, the kind with two wings and a weighted center. They flutter to the ground like a helicopter. One of those little things got into my car door and plugged the drainage hole at the bottom.

Looking at that little piece of plant matter, it didn't seem like a big deal, but it could have broken my whole car and cost me a lot of money. Removing it from the hole in my door cost almost nothing.

Do you ever hear a sloshing noise in your life? It's a warning. Something's building up. God wants to remove any little "helicopters" and drain stuff out before it short-circuits your life. Let me suggest some basic signs that show you probably haven't forgiven yet:

- Your thinking and judgment are clouded. Your thoughts seem to always be interrupted by something painful or irritating.

- Your service for Jesus is hindered. You won't give financially because the last place you gave mishandled your finances. You won't serve because you got hurt serving last time. On and on. Some people prefer online church because they don't want to do church with others. They want the safe place on the other side of a computer screen.

- The name of the person who hurt you is on your lips too often. He or she is too much at the top of your mind.

- You have a physical reaction when the person's name comes up. You feel nauseated and sick, endangered, and like you want to hide. Your heart races, and your thoughts tangle up like a train wreck.

- You have an unreal expectation of justice. You want God to be mad at the people you're mad at. You wonder why He won't strike the heathens down. You ask Him to strip them of every blessing. That defines your prayers for them.

- You produce bitter fruit from a bitter root. Your love, joy, and peace seem frozen. Instead your words are sarcastic and wounding. They tear down but don't build up.

GRACE FOR TODAY

Forgiveness needs to be exercised and managed. What does this look like?

It doesn't mean forgiving in advance for the next twenty years. That's impossible. Believe me; I've tried it. Rather, managing forgiveness means waking up and saying, "Just for today I choose forgiveness." Tomorrow you do the same thing. "Just for today..."

That's what it looks like. I like how the little girl misread the Lord's Prayer: "Forgive us our trash baskets, as we forgive those who put trash in our baskets." She was on to something. We make the choice to forgive each other's trash, just for today.

One time, I was in a restaurant and saw someone who had hurt me badly. To move in the opposite spirit of the pain that welled up in me, I secretly paid that person's bill. God will deal with the person for what he or she did. Last time I checked, revenge belonged to the Lord, not to Penny Maxwell or any other person.

I've noticed that when other people mess up, we call on God's justice, but when we mess up, we're a big fan of His mercy. I can't remember one time when I messed up and went to the Lord and said, "I blew it, Lord. Would You pour hot coals on my head? Would You remove Your blessings from me? Please make me pay for everything I've done." I don't do that regarding my sin, but I do for others'. We judge ourselves by our intentions and other people by their actions. Our standard should be uniform all the way around.

And as I said, I've also proven personally that we can't store up grace.

When I was getting ready to have my second child, I thought, "How am I going to do this? I already have one child. How can I possibly do everything that needs to be done in a day?"

God told me, "You're wanting to store up grace, but

you can't do that." He reminded me of the Israelites gathering manna. They didn't understand how God worked. He wanted to teach them a principle by having them wake up every day and come look for His provision—and for Him. They wanted to keep trusting and relying on their own strength, which took them into fear and greed, and they went out to gather more than they needed for that day. It never worked—the extra manna became full of worms after one day (or two days when it was the Sabbath).

Why wouldn't God let them gather for weeks in advance? It was a principle: every day we have to choose God again. Every day we come to Him for provision, for relationship, or for whatever we need. So many of us want to plot our path through the pain. God wants us to wake up every day and trust Him for that day. Tomorrow you do the same thing. The day after do the same thing. His mercies are new every morning. The Bible says that today is the day of salvation (2 Cor. 6:2), meaning we should live in the now. Jesus said each day has enough trouble of its own, so don't worry about tomorrow (Matt. 6:34). It's a process of learning to lean on God, a mental pattern and a lifestyle we must develop.

INHERITING WELL

This prepares us to dwell successfully in our promised land. When your immediate crisis is over and your wilderness is behind you, if you didn't learn the lesson of daily grace, then you won't trust God. You will wake up every day wondering if the promised land will be taken from you or if something might rob you of the abundance there. Managing forgiveness is not just about getting to the place you want to be; it's about sustaining and prospering there.

If God gives you the marriage or child you wanted, but you haven't learned to trust God for fresh mercies every morning, you will wrestle with evil foreboding like I did: "Oh my gosh, what if my marriage doesn't work out? What if our child dies? What if I lose the job?" Grace for today means turning that thought around and saying, "God is going to bless me today in ways I don't even know about. I'm going to find God this morning when I search for Him." Even if you have a bad day or something painful happens, you can say, "There's a new day tomorrow and fresh mercies for me when I wake up." It liberates you from the past and the future.

Jesus could have saved grace up if anyone could have, but the night before His death He was wrestling mightily with what was just ahead. The day had its own trouble that He couldn't get rid of in advance. He had to walk in the same grace we do for our problems.

So every day, I get up and put on God's love. There's not a day I don't have that option. Every day, I wake up and choose faith over fear. I go out and gather just enough for today. I live in 2 Corinthians 12:10, which says, "When I am weak, then I am strong." I live in 2 Corinthians 10:5, which has been a key for my healing. It says we must continually take thoughts captive, casting down high things that exalt themselves against the knowledge of God. I constantly challenge my internal dialogue when it doesn't line up with the Word. I don't allow a negative thought to go unchallenged. Every day—and I do mean every—when a negative thought pops to mind, I do my best to immediately arrest it and remove it from the garden of my mind.

I can testify that these habits produce abundant, beneficial fruit for myself and others.

LETTING SOME BONES BREAK

There is also a sense in which we cannot always help people avoid broken bones. Each one of us has to learn these principles for ourselves—sometimes the hard way.

Our youngest child, Cassidy, had some years when she hung out with questionable people in high school, and at times she started to shut us out and exclude us from her life. Troy and I did not coddle our kids or stand on the sidelines like a referee, blowing a whistle every time they approached danger. We knew there were some consequences they needed to experience for themselves. Troy and I had such traumatic upbringings that we were forced to be strong. Our kids got to avoid a lot of painful stuff, so we intentionally let them go through some difficult things because we didn't want them to grow up weak.

One day, Cassidy skipped school and thought she had pulled one over on the principal and on us. But I found out about it, picked up the phone, and called the principal, who was a good friend of ours and loved our church.

"I want you to know that Cassidy skipped school and was off the campus," I said. "She will probably try it again."

"All right," he said. "Don't tell her that you called me. I'm going to call her down to my office."

He did and told her he had caught her leaving school on the surveillance cameras. She received an in-school suspension, and to her credit she came home and told me about it. I played dumb and was like, "Oh really?" I was glad to let her get a taste of negative consequences for that.

Later, when she graduated, I told her I had informed the principal, and she burst out, "I wondered if you did!"

In other ways too we had to let her hit potholes, bust her tires, and learn lessons herself. We decided that road bumps are OK. Dead ends are not. Cassidy made it through those. She outgrew teenage rebellion and went to college, and I'm glad she doesn't have the level of broken bones Troy and I did, but she sure learned from the ones she got. That has made her a much better person than if we had spared her from all hurt and disappointment.

She understood for herself that God resets anything that breaks.

CHAPTER 10

THE POWER IN YOUR FREEDOM

MY DAD'S FUNERAL was not much of a celebration. He had at least twelve children he had fathered by various women. The ones that were there that day were angry—not at his death but at him for not being there for any of them. Because I let God reset that bone of abandonment, I had a sense of joy where my half-siblings were mired in pain.

"Why aren't you angry?" they asked me.

"Because I lowered my expectation of him and raised my expectation of God," I told them.

There was another reason too. I had ministered to my dad on his deathbed and led him to the Lord. That moment would have been impossible if I hadn't let God reset the broken bone of his negligence and abandonment of me as a child. My freedom became my dad's freedom. The salvation I received he received too. We both became children of mercy.

At his funeral I spoke and gave a call for people to come to the Lord. If my wound of fatherlessness had been unhealed, I never could have shared the gospel as I did. When we get healed, it produces healing in others as well.

MIMI'S LAST REPENTANCE

Troy's grandmother Mimi had reached the end of her life and was confined to a bed; she couldn't move. Mimi was sweet and loving right up to the end. For years before she lost her mobility, she would sit in the front row of our church, beaming with pride for her grandson. She was without a doubt our biggest fan. Knowing it was painful for her to sit in the hard chairs we used for our then-mobile church, we put out a big, comfortable chair for her when she visited. Any woman in her nineties surely deserved special treatment.

When she became completely bedridden, we visited her weekly and then daily in the nursing home. They categorized her condition as a failure to thrive. Every visit was potentially a last visit with her.

Normally we visited her separately—Troy alone or me with the children. One day by happenstance we went together as a family and were standing at her bedside when Troy said bluntly, "Mimi, I feel like there are things you need to ask forgiveness for before you die."

I was stunned. "The woman watches *Jeopardy!* and lies in this bed! What in the world?" I thought but kept quiet for the time being.

"Mimi, is there anything you need confess?" Troy continued.

I couldn't help it; I swung an elbow at him, thinking, "Confess? What are you talking about? What kind of sin are you asking an old, bedridden woman to confess?"

By this time Mimi couldn't speak anymore, so we were looking for signs of her reaction to the things Troy was saying. To my surprise she nodded her head slightly to indicate, "Yes."

"I really feel like there's a lack of forgiveness," Troy said. "Have certain things been bothering you?"

She nodded her head slightly again. I was no longer throwing elbows at my husband and was indeed surprised at how this was going.

"You are holding on to guilt and unforgiveness," Troy stated. "Mimi, I turned out well. I'm living a good life and preaching the gospel. Don't burden your heart with all of that regret anymore."

Little tears formed in her eyes, and she was squeezing his hand. It seemed she had held pain in her heart for all of these years because her son, Troy's dad, had betrayed her and lived such a self-serving life. She paid his child support the whole time Troy was a child because Troy's dad never would. He stole money, jewelry, and valuables from her to pay for his alcohol. He was in and out of jail for DUIs. Eventually his license was suspended permanently. He then got drunk and fell off a horse, suffering major head trauma. He was her only child. Troy was her only grandchild.

The disaster I thought was developing in that nursing home room turned into a sweet and significant moment in Mimi's life. It reminded me of an encounter in the Bible that always bothered me. Jesus approached a paralyzed man in Jerusalem, healed him, and commanded him, "Sin no more" (John 5:14, esv). When reading that, I always thought, "It's not like the guy is sleeping around or stealing from his neighbors. He's paralyzed! What the heck?"

Mimi's response showed me that even the most vulnerable and needy can harbor resentment toward others. In the paralyzed man's case he was clearly upset that others had gotten their healing before he did. Who knows what kind of bitterness and anger toward God resided in the man's heart that Jesus sought to heal?

Mimi died not long after that day at her bedside. We had a funeral for her in Richmond, where she was from, and all her old friends came. She had touched many lives through her generosity and service on missionary boards and church organizations. Everybody loved Mimi.

Two weeks after she died, Troy's dad died, having been in a hospital for a long time and destroyed his body with drugs and alcohol. Troy went down to the empty apartment in Florida where his dad had spent his last days. It was void of furniture but for a single chair. Troy found handwritten notes his father had left, detailing the kind of memorial service he wanted to have. It involved a big celebration with his old rock band and a lot of plans so grand as to be sad. None of it happened, and few regretted that he was gone. Such was the contrast of a mother and son who had lived such different lives from each other.

Because Troy bravely offered Mimi a last opportunity to heal her soul, even on her deathbed, she ended her life free of unforgiveness. His freedom had multiplied.

AWAKENED TO INTERCEDE

As we walked in forgiveness and freedom from broken bones, it amazed me how available it made us to do assignments for the Lord. Instead of being all wrapped up in our own hurts, we were on call to help others.

One night at 2:30 a.m. I was sound asleep when the Holy Spirit woke me up abruptly. I can't explain it any other way. I knew immediately that I was supposed to go downstairs and pray.

"Where are you going?" Troy asked as I got out of bed.

"I've got to go pray," I said. This was not typical behavior for me, but I felt compelled to do it. I knelt by our couch downstairs and for half an hour or so prayed in the Spirit. English just didn't seem like enough. After that amount of time I felt a peace and a sense of completion come over me, so I went back upstairs and back to bed.

I had just laid my head down when I heard this awful, vicious-sounding noise from what seemed to be some distance away. I was immediately sure it had awakened everyone within a mile or two. Troy bolted upright.

"What was that?" he exclaimed. My response to his question baffled even me.

"Quick, go down there!" I told him. "It's our neighbor. He's been drinking and has been in a car accident. He wrapped his car around a tree, and you're going to be the first one on site. He needs help."

"What are you talking about?" my husband replied. We didn't know our neighbor or his family that well. I had no knowledge of his having a drinking problem.

"I don't know, but put your sweatpants on and get down there!" I insisted.

Troy sensed the authority in what I was saying and did exactly what I commanded. Sometime later he came back and said, "How in the world did you know what had happened?" Everything was exactly as I had described it. Troy had stayed with our neighbor until the paramedics came.

I knew what had happened: the Holy Spirit kept our neighbor alive through prayers of intercession. A couple of days later, after he got out of the hospital, I went down and told him and his family what had happened, and they met Jesus.

SHIPWRECKED

Your freedom is meant to be shared. It is meant to spare other people harm.

In Acts 27 Paul, a prisoner, was taken by ship into stormy seas. Paul had a sense this would go badly, and he warned his Roman guard and the ship's captain that they would suffer much loss if they ventured into uncertain waters. They ignored Paul and sailed anyway.

The storm that came upon them got so bad that for two weeks, none of the 276 people on the ship saw the sun or moon. Rather, they all gave up hope of surviving. Paul, suffering this same uncertainty, then was visited by an angel who promised that all lives would be spared, but all the cargo would be lost. Why was God sparing their lives? Because of Paul's presence and intercession. The angel told him, "God has graciously given you the lives of all who sail with you" (v. 24).

Paul's freedom became their freedom. This freedom continued to spread.

Everyone swam or floated to shore. It was raining, so Paul, being industrious and helpful, gathered wood to make a fire for their survival. While he was doing this kind act, a venomous viper, driven out by the heat, fastened itself to Paul's hand.

Pause right there. If I'm Paul, I'm having a conversation with God that goes something like: "I told them not to go on this journey. They did anyway, and I suffered along with them. Then we're shipwrecked, and it's raining. I try to build a fire for everyone and get bit by a poisonous snake. God, why wouldn't You protect me?"

This is such a clear picture of what happens to some of us with broken bones. Every new pain—every viper from the fire—sends us into the poor-me song. "Look at this viper attached to my hand. Can you believe it after all I've done for God?"

But God was working in this situation to bring freedom to others. Instead of letting that viper stick to his hand and pump poison into him while he sat there with his lip quivering, feeling all sorry for himself, Paul instead shook it off. In other words, he wasn't going to let that poison into his bloodstream. He knew better than to dwell on that pain.

Of course things got worse right after that. Rumors started among the islanders who said, "No doubt this man is a murderer, whom, though he has escaped the sea, yet justice does not allow to live" (Acts 28:4, NKJV). Talk about piling it on.

But because of these unusual circumstances and the healing power of Jesus through Paul, God brought island-wide revival. Everything turned around. Paul's pain—and Paul's freedom from bitterness—saved the lives of 276 people on the boat and saved the souls of countless hundreds or thousands on that island.

That's how God works.

SOUP KITCHEN TESTIMONY

One time, when we were new to the city and our church was still meeting in a rundown elementary school, I was invited to be one of the speakers at the opening of a soup kitchen in Charlotte. A lot of people showed up for this dedication, and when I saw that the other speaker was a well-known pastor in Charlotte and had a family legacy there, I wondered, "Why am I here? What do I bring that this guy doesn't?" I was pretty sure the answer was, "Nothing."

This seemed to prove true when he got up to speak. He was so engaging and nice, tall, and manly, and he came from such great ministry stock. He talked about how the faithfulness of his father, a pastor, was the reason this kitchen was being dedicated. It was his father's dream. He discussed his lineage in ministry, how his father would call him every day before dying recently. He read this from his father's obituary, and it was just amazing.

I was sitting there waiting to speak, thinking, "This is the sweetest, nicest guy, with such a history of family character, honor, and integrity. Here's me: My dad was a player, and my parents had eight marriages between them. I have a broken past and no proven ministry in Charlotte. Dear God, why am I here today? I come from the underbelly of society. This man's church has campuses all over Charlotte, and our meeting place's roof is leaky, and we use offering buckets to catch the rain."

Too soon he sat down, and I did my duty and got up to speak.

"Everything you just heard, I came from the complete opposite," I said, figuring there is nothing like the truth. "My mom and dad were married eight different times to various people. My dad still ran around on his fifth wife and had girlfriends on the side. I never had a relationship with him and haven't spoken to my mother in fifteen years. But God can use anybody, and I'm glad He called me—because I didn't have a lineage, but I get to start a lineage."

I then talked about how God healed my childhood traumas and is able to turn anybody's story around. I said the church needs both kinds of stories: those who relate to the great lineage of the other speaker and those who relate to mine.

Believe it or not, when I finished and sat down, the Lord rebuked the daylights out of me. He said, "Who called you? Did not I call you?" He was not pleased that I had placed such an emphasis on my dysfunctional family, as if this presented a barrier to God working through me. All I could say under my breath was, "You're right, Lord!"

The man running the event got up and said, "I'm going to have these two pastors stand up front and offer prayer for anyone who wants to come up." I literally stood there with my head bowed and eyes closed saying, "OK, Lord, You called me, but if I just heard how dysfunctional I am and how perfect the other pastor is, I wouldn't get prayer from me. Who's going to get into my line?"

I waited, looking at my shoes, and soon saw another pair of shoes step into view. Keeping my head down out of shame more than humility, I prayed for the person. Then another pair of shoes stepped into view. Glancing up, I saw a big line weaving through the auditorium for people wanting to receive prayer from me. I don't say this to be disrespectful, but there was not a single person in the other pastor's line. It was as if the Lord was making a point to me: "Don't you ever question your calling again."

I never have.

CONCLUSION

OUR FAMILY HAD a tradition when the kids were young. Whenever Troy or I drove away from the house, the kids stood in the bay window waving and jumping up and down. We flashed our headlights at them, honked, and waved back. It was an extra "I love you" on our way out somewhere. If we forgot to do it, they would call us immediately, and we had to drive back, flash our lights, and leave again the right way. It was one of many ways we stayed close and enjoyed one another.

After Colby's car accident I felt as if our family healed up well. Colby's confidence needed rebuilding, of course. When we got home that afternoon, he stated flatly, "I don't want to drive again."

"You don't have to for a few days, but after that we want you behind the wheel again," I told him. "We'll be with you."

We didn't want him gripped by fear, and in good time he was driving without fear again.

The biggest thing for me was continuing to own my

thoughts in the morning before they could go down the wrong road. I wasn't really afraid that Colby or my daughters would have a car accident, but I didn't take any chances. I tuned the instrument every morning, thanking God for that day and for His protection, then waking up the next day and doing it all over again. The decision I made on the side of the road in the sight of God held firmly. One of my reminders was a small piece of glass from Colby's car that I kept in a drawer with a lot of other mementos. On the glass was a sliver of a Freedom House bumper sticker that had been on his car. It took its place among things in that drawer, like the belt Troy wore on our first date, my kids' school IDs, Colby's football jersey, my daughters' corsages from their father-daughter dances—and the positive pregnancy tests for each of the children.

The day came when Colby moved out to attend Bible college in Virginia. He would be my first to leave the nest. Troy was going to drive him up there— I knew it would wreck me to leave and come back with an empty car—and though Colby would only be five or six hours away, feelings of loss came back stronger than at any time since the accident. My first-born was going off into the world. How would it treat him? Would he still want to call home and talk to Mom? What would he experience? Would the good outweigh the bad?

Would he get his own broken bones?

Colby and his dad crammed the remaining items

into the car, we hugged, and then I was the one standing in the bay window, waving and watching the car pull away. The lights flickered; the horn honked. I watched them disappear into the distance, and in my heart I went back to the moment on the hill when the Lord had done such a hard thing with me among the wrecked cars that day.

"Yes, Lord," I said anew. "I trust You. I trust You with who he is. I trust You with him. I trust You with his life."

I turned and walked into the rest of the house where my daughters were enjoying a new sense of ownership and expanded space. I knew that no matter what happened, everything would be all right. We're not in that perfect garden anymore. We have to deal with things, but we have a perfect Savior, who promises to be there with us in our imperfect situations.

No matter what happens, God always resets our broken bones when we let Him.

EPILOGUE

I WAS SITTING AT a conference some years ago, and Lisa Bevere, a friend of mine, was speaking. I heard the Lord literally say the words "setting broken bones" to me.

"That should be the title for Lisa's book!" I thought excitedly.

But when I told her, she wasn't convinced. After a while she put it back on me, and I realized it was supposed to be the title for my book.

Walking through healing is an *-ing* not an *-ed*. It's hardly ever past tense. It's ongoing. We stay in shape. We go in for regular checkups. It's important to be willing to be investigated by God to see if there's anything that's not the way it should be. Psalm 139:23–24 says, "Search me, God, and know my heart; test me and know my anxious thoughts. See if there is any offensive way in me, and lead me in the way everlasting."

God is not about perfection but about progress. He wants us to hit markers of maturity. Maybe it's noticing that things that used to bother you don't anymore. Things that used to create wounds just bounce off now. I like to say that your scars show you have a past, but Jesus' scars show you have a future.

I end with one of my favorite quotes, which is a blessing: "Now to him who is able to do immeasurably more than all we ask or imagine, according to his power that is at work within us, to him be glory in the church and in Christ Jesus throughout all generations, for ever and ever! Amen" (Eph. 3:20–21).

NOTES

Chapter 7

1. Blue Letter Bible, s.v. *"pneuma,"* accessed August 18, 2021, https://www.blueletterbible.org/lexicon/g4151/kjv/tr/0-1/; Blue Letter Bible, s.v. *"pythōn,"* accessed August 18, 2021, https://www.blueletterbible.org/lexicon/g4436/kjv/tr/0-1/.

2. Dutch Sheets, "Day 31, Chapter 30: The Price," Give Him 15, June 7, 2021, https://www.givehim15.com/post/june-7-2021/.